CHILDREN'S COGNITIVE DEVELOPMENT

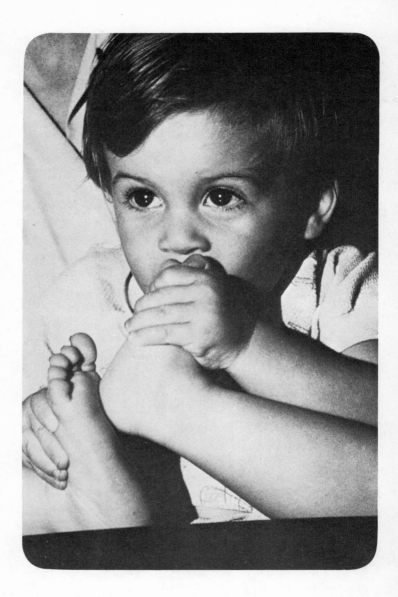

CHILDREN'S COGNITIVE DEVELOPMENT

PIAGET'S THEORY
AND THE PROCESS APPROACH

by
RUTH L. AULT
University of Utah

New York
OXFORD UNIVERSITY PRESS
1977

The author acknowledges the kind permission of authors and publishers to redraw original art work:

M. Levine, "Hypothesis behavior by humans during discrimination learning." *Journal of Experimental Psychology,* 1966, *71,* p. 331. Copyright © 1966 by the American Psychological Association. Reprinted by permission.

P. R. Kingsley and J. W. Hagen, "Induced vs. spontaneous rehearsal in short-term memory in nursery school children." *Developmental Psychology,* 1969, *1,* p. 41. Copyright © 1969 by the American Psychological Association. Reprinted by permission.

R. Gelman, "Conservation acquisition: A problem of learning to attend to relevant attributes." *Journal of Experimental Child Psychology,* 1969, *7,* p. 174. Copyright © 1969 by Academic Press. Reprinted by permission.

Illustrations by Fred Winkowski

Since I had a purpose and readership in mind when I wrote this book, I ought to share that information with you, the reader. This book was designed as a supplement to college courses in child development, particularly as taught in Psychology departments, but also including Educational Psychology, Family Life, and Nursing departments in which an unspecialized course in child development is taught. The target audience is, therefore, undergraduate with not necessarily more than an Introductory Psychology course as a prerequisite. Why read a supplement at all? A glance through child psychology texts provides the answer. A majority of such texts emphasizes the child's physical and social development, relegating cognitive development to a secondary role. Often a single chapter covers both Piaget's theory and information about standardized intelligence testing. The topics of memory and perception are frequently missing or presented disjointedly. In few cases is there any attempt to compare or contrast the Piagetian approach with the approach of the non-Piagetian experimental child psychology (called the *process approach* in this book). This book, then, seeks to remedy that situation. It has been kept short enough to function as a supplement to full-length child psychology texts but is long enough to fill in the bare sketch of cognitive development painted in the primary texts. Although other cognitively oriented supplements exist, they are primarily introductions to Piaget's theory alone and are deeper treatments than is desirable for general introductory courses.

This text has a dual orientation, presenting both Piaget's theory and the research efforts of experimental child psychologists who have cognitive, but not necessarily Piagetian, interests. Such an orientation requires the presentation of research results in somewhat greater detail than is common at the introductory level. Having taught child psychology for several years, I know that the mention of research can produce sheer panic in some students. Puzzled by complicated research designs and arcane statistical analyses, introductory (and many advanced) students shy away from experimental psychology. My intention is to bring research findings to the reader in an intelligible and as nontechnical a fashion as possible. For me, that meant describing enough about an experiment that the reader would understand both its results and their significance. This contrasts with the usual treatment of listing one-sentence summaries of the results, which end up being viewed as isolated facts to be memorized. An intelligible presentation also meant excluding statistics, ignoring aspects of experiments that were tangential to the point being discussed, and avoiding the technical jargon of experimental psychology. The advantage over a book of readings that reprints journal articles is clear. For the advanced reader, reference citations indicate sources of further information: original sources in the case of journal articles and other books in the case of Piaget's theory.

The reader should also note that this book has been liberally sprinkled with footnotes. Like all good footnotes, those in this book are tangential to the basic information of the main presentation. Some provide slightly more technical information that the advanced reader may wish to pursue. Others are what I consider to be humorous asides.* I hope the reader will read them.

I also hope that the reader will find this book both useful and enjoyable, for those were my two goals in writing it. Although it is certainly not a layman's guide to parenting or educating children, it is intended to be helpful to any-

---

* Or snide remarks, depending on one's perspective.

one who has contact with the younger members of our species. The underlying philosophy is that a basic under-standing of normal cognitive development should help make interactions with children more sensible and, conse-quently, more pleasant.

Before I started this work, I read the prefaces of many other books. I was continually skeptical of the acknowledg-ment section, wondering how the author ever cajoled (or conned) so many of his colleagues into reading endless drafts of the manuscript. Having now written this book, I am amazed at, and eternally grateful for, the number who helped me. Encouragement came from faculty, students, secretaries, and friends alike. In particular, I wish to thank Donna Gelfand, Donald Hartmann, Joan Lessen-Firestone, Cindy Cromer, Christine Mitchell, and Lizette Peterson for their highly useful and detailed comments on manuscript drafts. Irwin Altman, David Dodd, and Marigold Linton helped prepare me for my initial contact with publishers (a bewildering business for novices). Janine Seely and Judie Turner served as able typists. Friends and their children provided many of the delightful anecdotes I have re-counted here, but I suspect they wish to remain anony-mous.

Finally, I wish to thank my husband. Not only did he suffer through the normal trials and tribulations of a spouse whose partner is writing a book, but he also tolerated such unreasonable demands as thinking up stories to illustrate some point I wished to make (usually by counterarguing that *he* did not have many years of experience studying children and mine *ought* to suffice). After laughing hysteri-cally at my initial sketches, he drew the figures for the man-uscript draft submitted to the publisher.* He also cheer-fully read draft after draft, providing insightful comments

---

* His laughter was quite justified, I might add.

vii

and encouragement. In return for these considerations, he demanded that I become a successful author and support him in the style to which he wanted to become accustomed. A fair bargain to my way of thinking.

R.L.A.

Salt Lake City
January, 1976

CONTENTS

CHILDREN'S COGNITIVE DEVELOPMENT

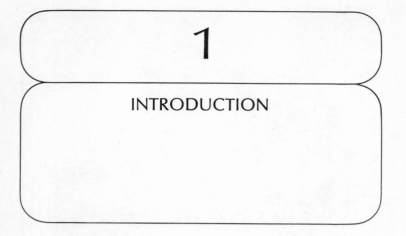

1

INTRODUCTION

Four-year-old Susan was asked where she got her name. She answered, "My mommy named me." "What if your mother had called you Jack?" "Then, I'd be a boy." To many children, names embody certain other characteristics; if one has a boy's name, then one must have other features making one male. Susan also claimed that if the name of the sun were changed and it was called the moon, "then it would be dark in the daytime."

A three-year-old girl, with a gleam in her eye, approached a plant. Her mother cautioned her not to touch it. "Why not?" "Because you might hurt it." "No, I won't, 'cause it can't cry." She associated crying with hurting and denied the possibility of the one without the other.

When asked to define "priceless," an eight-year-old guessed that it meant "something that's for free." Children tend to interpret words and expressions literally. (See Figure 1-1.)

These are just some of the numerous examples of how children's thinking is different from the thinking of adults. The study of cognitive development brings out these differences in thinking and how they change as children grow

"Curiosity killed the cat."

older. The practical implication of cognitive development is clear. How a child thinks, and how his* thinking changes as he develops, has an obvious impact on his behavior at home and on what he learns at school. In addition to the practical significance, studying children's thinking can be fascinating and fun. Although the expression beginning

* Of course half of all children are "she's" and not "he's," but the English language is not well suited to referring to a single child without assigning sex. In this book references to a child as "he" are presumed to include "she." Similarly, parents and teachers will generally be labeled female with all due apologies to fathers and male instructors.

4

"Billy caught 40 winks."

Figure 1-1. Proverbs and metaphors conjure up childish mental images.

"out of the mouths of babes" usually refers to the honesty with which children speak, it also serves to remind us that children say what they think and their thinking can be amusingly different.

The purpose of this book is to describe briefly the course of cognitive development. The description will take two forms because psychologists have studied cognitive development by two different methods. The most complete and unified theory of cognitive development has come from the method of naturalistic observation, employed most notably by Jean Piaget, a Swiss psychologist. In a naturalistic observation, the investigator watches and records whatever happens as the child goes about his daily activities. The second method of study, laboratory experimentation, has been used by many different investigators. Although none of them has proposed a single comprehensive theory like Piaget's, they share a common approach, investigating processes of thought, so their work will be referred to as the *process approach*. In the laboratory experiment, the child is taken to a special room (often alone) and asked to perform a specific task. The investigator assesses the child's performance, either according to some predetermined standard or relative to the performance of other children.

Each method has advantages and disadvantages. If a naturalistic observation is to be thorough, the investigator must have daily access to his subjects for long portions of the day. Since even close family friends are unwilling to tolerate such intrusions into their lives, investigators typically observe their own children. That increases the chances that the observer will be biased in his recording and in his interpreting of the events that he sees. Even the most objective of observers occasionally yields to the temptation to regard his own children as little angels. It is also difficult for the observer to refrain from participating in, and thereby influencing, the course of events. It is the rare observer who can remain passive when the child's curiosity leads him to investigate the properties of matches. The enormous time demands of the observational method usually limit the study to a few children. The observer then cannot determine whether some phenomenon is peculiar to the few children in the observation or whether it has more widespread generality. Conclusions drawn from small sample observations are, therefore, open to the criticism that they are not applicable to broad ranges of children.

In contrast, laboratory experiments are purposely designed to be less biased and more general than observations. They are less biased because the person who tests the children is typically unfamiliar with any of the subjects and often does not even know the purpose of the experiment. Laboratory experiments permit greater generality because large numbers of children can be tested. An additional advantage stems from systematic manipulations of the environment. Scientific statements of cause and effect can only be made when the experimenter has controlled the presence or absence of some treatments and has obtained systematic effects as a result. In observations, the investigator can describe factors as they occur, but he cannot rule out alternative causal explanations such as maturation or prior events without measuring and contrasting groups of children. Laboratory experiments can suffer, however, from artificiality and narrowness of scope. The laboratory setting establishes a contrived situation that may induce the children to behave in an unusual manner, and because only one small facet of the child's thinking processes is studied at a time, the interrelations between processes are difficult to investigate. Observations are much richer in portraying the whole child.

The laboratory experiment and the naturalistic observation each provides data that the other cannot; each is a valuable method for adding to our knowledge about children. Chapters 2 and 3 in this book exemplify these two methodologies as they have been applied to the study of cognitive development. Corresponding to the observational and experimental methods are two ways to organize the collected information about children. A naturalistic observer studies all facets of the same child's behavior as that child develops, so it is not surprising that the results of these observations tend to be organized *by ages or stages*. All of the child's cognitive skills are described for various times of his life, such as during infancy or adolescence. An experimentalist, on the other hand, usually studies the performance of many groups of children, often of different ages, on a small set of related tasks. These techniques suggest an organization *by process*. One particular problem-solving skill, e.g., memory, is discussed for all ages before the next skill, e.g., perception, is discussed. Neither organization is completely satisfactory for presenting cognitive development at the introductory level. If information is presented according to the age of the child, then the reader lacks a concise understanding of the development of a process because small parts of that process have been treated across ages. If the child's problem-solving skills are discussed as units (first one skill and then another), the reader has a poor comprehension of the child's capacities at any one moment in time. To adopt one organizational framework unfortunately relegates the other to a subsidiary status and makes the presentation of one of the methodologies difficult. Like the observational and experimental methods, both the age and process organizations offer valuable contributions to the study of cognitive development. Each of the next two chapters presents a single methodology and reflects its preferred organization.

OVERVIEW OF THE REMAINING CHAPTERS

Chapter 2 presents the theory of Jean Piaget. His primary method was to observe the development of his own three children. In presenting his theory we shall adopt his stage organization. Piaget has performed some experiments, but in them he tended to use only a few subjects and often omitted the control techniques typical of the experimental method. This lack of experimental rigor, combined with the general problems of the observational technique, has led many American psychologists to criticize Piaget's work for its lack of objectivity and generality. In spite of these objections, his writings are rich and compelling descriptions of very real children and they have stimulated a considerable amount of research.

Chapter 3 presents a compilation of the results of the experimental child psychology research tradition. We shall adopt a process organization of this material as suggested by Jerome Kagan. It will become apparent that many different experimenters have researched a wide variety of cognitive processes. No one theory fits all the pieces together, so the account may seem disjointed, but it is a valid representation of the data accumulated from research.

Because results are more understandable when the experimental procedures are also understood, brief descriptions of many experiments are presented in Chapters 2 and 3. The reader without much background in psychology should rest assured that the presentations are simplified and technical jargon has been avoided as much as possible. For the more advanced reader, reference citations indicate the original sources to which the reader can turn for more detailed information.

Although in some instances research and observation produce conflicting results, more often the data are complementary. Chapter 4 indicates just a few of the similarities and some unresolved differences which arise from Piaget's observations and the experimental research.

The fifth and final chapter is an attempt to make the preceding chapters relevant to parents and educators. It exemplifies how adults can evaluate a problem-solving task in terms of the demands placed on the child's capacity to think. The underlying philosophy for this book is that each child is unique, has an individual rate of development, and has an individual set of needs. Hence, no one list of specific suggestions will suit the various situations that parents and educators meet daily in their interactions with children. Chapter 5, therefore, is not a comprehensive manual on child-rearing or child-educating. Nor can it be a compendium of useful suggestions for the distraught parent or teacher. Instead, it proposes that adults create their own list of solutions based on an assessment of the child's current level of cognitive development and of the task demands.

In essence, the approach is to deny two popular ideas: the concept of the "average" child and the "correct" way to handle children. The average child is as mythical as the unicorn. No person has ever seen one. His characteristics are assigned according to whatever statistical average results from measuring a sample of children. Real children have unique clusters of abilities, some above and some below the average. What is a description of the average child will not necessarily describe any one particular child.

Similarly, if each child is unique, then no one way of handling a situation can be uniformly right or wrong. Wise advice-givers must always hedge their bets. They rarely have as much information about the specific situation as the advice-seeker and so cannot make as informed a judgment. They can, however, tell the advice-seeker what factors might be weighed in the decision. That is the function of this book's final chapter.

It is always difficult to decide how to limit the topics under consideration, especially since the maxim "everything always relates to everything else" is particularly appropriate for the psychology of human organisms. The determining factors in this book are a combination of personal bias, traditional lines of psychological inquiry, interest for the reader, and availability of research findings, but not necessarily in that order. The contents of this book are also determined by two major assumptions concerning the child and his developing processes: that the child is active and that his behavior is determined by an interaction of biology and the environment.

ASSUMPTION 1: THE ACTIVE CHILD

We assume that the child is an *active* rather than a passive participant in his own development. This assumption means that the child is not merely a passive recipient of whatever environmental stimulation happens to impinge upon him. Rather, he actively seeks certain types of stimulation and avoids others. For example, he looks at the bars of his crib rather than at the middle of his mattress. He focuses on his mother's eyes instead of on her ears. He turns his head toward the sound of his mother's voice, but he does not turn toward the window when the lawn mower passes by. In being active, the child helps to determine what behaviors he will exhibit. A ten-month-old may babble sounds like *maah, mmmah, mahmah, may, mey, meh,* etc. until he can produce the particular sound he desires or until he masters and controls his own behavior.

This position does not deny the importance of environmental stimuli in shaping the child's behavior. Consider again the ten-month-old babbling. Research has shown that American babies will tend, over time, to babble sounds more and more like those the child will need in speaking English, and less like the sounds produced by Russian or Japanese children. The environment must be influencing the child to result in this language shaping. By the same token, the child contributes to the process too. He exercises some choice regarding how much time to spend babbling and whether to work on the *ma* syllable or the *da* one.

The assumption of an active child implies that the child inherently tries to make sense out of his environment. If certain experiences will help the child figure out a problem, then the child will seek out those experiences. As soon as he has figured out the solution (to his own satisfaction), he will turn his attention to other matters. In other words, a child is active because he has an intrinsic motivation to learn about his world. How does a child decide which of the numerous problems confronting him to solve? The *moderate novelty principle* proposes that a person's attention is attracted to events that are mildly different from the old. Events that are completely familiar are boring; events that are too discrepant from the familiar are either unintelligible or frightening. Hence the child turns to moderately novel problems.

ASSUMPTION 2: THE INTERACTIONIST POSITION

When a behavior is universal, occurring in virtually every human being, one can postulate that the behavioral sequence is innate—a wired-in aspect of our nervous system. This position, called *nativism,* occupies one extreme of the spectrum. The people who advocate nativism are frequently called maturationists because they believe that behavior stems from simple, physical maturation of the organism living in a minimal environment (one containing oxygen and food). At the other extreme of the spectrum are the empiricists, who postulate that some experiences are so pervasive that all people are exposed to them in every known culture. The empiricist position is advocated by environmentalists (not to be confused with conservationists) since they believe that behaviors are learned as a result of experience with the environment, given a minimally working physical body (an intact brain and spinal cord). In between the two extremes is a wide range of positions reflecting varying degrees of *interaction* between the forces of mother nature (maturation) and of nurture (learning). Interactionists maintain that the biological and cultural aspects of a person's life are so intertwined that it is difficult, and frequently meaningless, to try to separate the impact of these two forces.

Indeed, there are some cultural experiences so pervasive that all children are exposed to them. For example, all infants are fed by someone else, or they do not survive. There are also some universal innate behavioral sequences. All healthy infants cry when pricked by a pin. Most behavior, however, results from a combination of inherent predispositions and environmentally determined experiences. The interactionist position is advocated by nearly all psychologists today and is the second major assumption of this book. Nevertheless, there are many different types of interactionists, depending on how much a single factor is emphasized and another given secondary consideration. As you shall read, Piaget has been interpreted as giving more weight to biological constraints, and the experimental tradition has been more interested in the role of experience.

Corresponding to the three positions (maturation, environmental experience, and their interaction) are three terms, each of which describes a change in behavior over time. *Growth* is that change which arises from physical maturation of the body. *Learning* is change due to contact with some environmental experience. *Development,* the most general change, is a function of both maturation and experience. Thus, when a change in behavior is labeled as growth, learning, or development, the cause of the change has been implicitly stated as maturation, environmental experience or their interaction, respectively. The reader should recall these implicit causes whenever these terms occur. The title of this book, *Children's Cognitive Development,* reflects its interactionist position.*

* Titles such as *Children's Learning* and *Studies in Cognitive Growth* were purposely avoided for two reasons: they might imply a learning or maturation orientation which would not be intended, and two excellent books already possess those titles, by Stevenson (1972) and by Bruner, Olver, and Greenfield (1966), respectively.

SUMMARY

The study of cognitive development is the study of how children's thinking changes over time and comes to be the thinking of adults. One method of studying cognitive development is through careful daily observations of children. Jean Piaget used this method, and the theory he proposed as a result of his observations is presented in Chapter 2. The organization of that material is by stages. Although both Piaget and the investigators whose research is presented in Chapter 3 are interactionists, Piaget placed more emphasis on maturation. The experimental research of Chapter 3 is more conveniently organized by processes of thinking. Because research is conducted on a large number of children, frequently of different ages, the impact of environmental experiences is more apparent, but the interactionist position is also maintained. Chapter 4 compares and contrasts some of the material from Chapters 2 and 3, while Chapter 5 indicates how the previous information can be used to help parents and teachers deal with children. The assumptions that a child is an active participant in his own development and that behavior stems from an interaction of growth and learning help limit and define the scope of this book.

2

PIAGET'S THEORY
OF COGNITIVE DEVELOPMENT

Jean Piaget has written extensively on various aspects of children's cognitive development. Since his theory is both comprehensive and complex, this brief introduction cannot do full justice to his theory. Only a few of the most basic terms and assumptions underlying Piaget's theory can be explained and only a cursory look can be taken of the developmental stages that Piaget proposed. More detailed information about Piaget's theory can be obtained from many excellent books, including Flavell (1963), Furth (1969), and Ginsburg and Opper (1969).

DEFINITION OF TERMS

Let us start our brief explanation of Piaget's theory by explaining one of the basic terms, *scheme,* which is an organized pattern of behavior. All of us engage in behavior patterns, or habits, which form part of our daily routine. Although we may never repeat any action exactly the same way, there is a similarity to the actions and it is possible to recognize the critical elements of the behavior pattern. To say that a child is sucking, for example, certain minimal criteria must be met. The cheeks and lips of the mouth must move in and out rhythmically in a drawing action, and some object, such as a thumb or nipple, is usually in the mouth. Other movements, such as the mouth opening and closing repeatedly, are the essential elements of other schemes, for example, biting. In sucking, it does not matter whether the child's right-hand thumb or left-hand thumb is in his mouth, or whether he brought his thumb to his mouth after scratching his cheek or after brushing hair out of his eyes. The essential ingredients of the scheme we are describing are the sucking movements. The object acted upon (right or left thumb) and the child's motivation for performing the action are environmental forces modifying any particular instance of a scheme. Piaget claims that the child, from earliest infancy, has many such schemes.

Two inherent tendencies govern how a person interacts with his environment. We shall describe these two tendencies in terms of the young child's behavioral schemes, but the tendencies also apply to the older child's *operations.* (Operations are the mental equivalents of behavioral schemes and will be discussed later in this chapter.) One of the two inherent tendencies is *organization.* Organization refers to the tendency to combine two or more discrete schemes into one higher order, smoother functioning scheme. Infants have several schemes such as grasping, sucking, and looking, which at first function independently. If someone places an object in an infant's palm, he will grasp the object. If an object appears in front of his eyes, he will look at it. But the infant who has not yet organized these two schemes will not perform the two behaviors simultaneously. With development (that is, with maturation and experience) the infant will come to look at things he grasps and grasp things he looks at.

The second inherent tendency is called *adaptation* and consists of two complementary processes: *assimilation* and *accommodation*. Assimilation involves the process of applying old schemes to new objects. Let us suppose that a child has the three schemes of grasping, biting, and shaking and now is confronted with a new object (say, a stuffed doll). He will try to understand this new object by applying his old schemes to it. He will grasp, bite, and shake the stuffed doll (hopefuly not disassembling it in the process). Thus, part of the child's adaptation to a new object is to assimilate it.*

The other part of the child's adaptation is to accommodate to the object's unique features. Accommodation involves modifying some elements of an old scheme or learning a new scheme that is more appropriate for the new object. The sucking scheme can be modified by drawing vigorously or weakly as a function of the size of the hole in the nipple. One of the properties of stuffed dolls is that they can be rubbed. Once the child learns to rub the doll, accommodation has occurred and he has learned a new scheme.†

Piaget's theory proposes that both assimilation and ac-

---

* A reader familiar with S-R learning theory might consider *assimilation* to be roughly analogous to the term *generalization*. Insofar as both terms imply that old responses are applied to new stimulus situations, the parallel certainly holds. *Generalization*, however, frequently connotes a lack of discrimination between stimuli, which *assimilation* does not connote.

† *Accommodation* can be viewed as analogous to *differentiation* in the sense that different responses are made to different stimuli.

commodation occur simultaneously whenever the child adapts to an environmental stimulus, but the particular balance between assimilation and accommodation can vary from situation to situation. Feedback from the environment is one important factor in determining which process is more influential. Other important factors include the extent to which the new stimulus situation differs from previous ones and on the kinds of schemes the child already has available. Let us consider again the example of the child who has been given the stuffed doll. When he applies his old schemes, he finds that grasping and shaking the stuffed doll do not produce very interesting noises. Biting stuffed dolls can be unpleasant (depending on the stuffing) so the child looks for new things to do with it and eventually comes upon rubbing. Accommodation has thus played a larger role than assimilation.

For a contrasting example let us suppose that the child has been given rattles before, with handles one-half inch in diameter or less. Then he is presented with a new rattle with a handle one inch in diameter. For the most part, the child will assimilate the new rattle, applying the old schemes of grasping and shaking it. He will have to accommodate only slightly. He must open his hand wider in order to grasp it, hold on harder, and shake with more force to produce any noise. In adapting to the new stimulus of a one-inch handle, assimilation has played a larger role than accommodation.

Piaget stated that there are two situations in which one form of adaptation takes definite precedence over the other. In make-believe play the child's behavior is predominantly assimilation. The child ignores the special features of a stimulus and responds to it as if it were something else. In many nursery schools, for example, a corner of the room is set up for playing house. Children can be seen sweeping the floor, washing dishes, setting the table, etc. The child who straddles the broom, pretending it is a flying vehicle, ignores the broom's sweeping capabilities and interacts with it as if it had wings. While we can look at such play as evidence of creativity, the child is not learning new schemes to help him interact with brooms as sweeping instruments. Imitation, on the other hand, is said to be primarily accommodation. The child learns a new scheme by imitating someone else's behaviors. When he observes his mother petting a dog and then imitates her behavior, he is accommodating to the dog. The dog could not be a completely novel object, however, because the child needs a framework to which he can connect the newly imitated behavior. Accommodation will not occur if the behavior to be imitated is too novel. Each time the child accommodates more than he assimilates, he adds to his repertoire of behaviors and becomes a bit more mature. In other words, advances in cognitive development are greater when accommodation plays a larger role than assimilation because the child's repertoire of behavior expands. Assimilation is still very important, though, because the child understands new objects by applying old schemes to them.

Although people of all ages have the two tendencies, organization and adaptation, an infant organizes and adapts differently from a younger child, an older child, or an adult. This is because the types of behaviors a person exhibits in one stage of development change as a result of biological maturation and experience with the environment. Some behavior patterns are thought to be important enough and different enough from the preceding ones to warrant being considered the defining characteristics of a distinct stage of development. Various translations of Piaget's books have differed in calling these time divisions stages or periods. We shall adopt the terminology that *stages* are basic divisions of development and that *periods* are broader time blocks frequently incorporating several stages within them. Any theory that uses stages to describe development will be called a *stage theory*. Piaget's stage theory identified four major periods of cognitive development which we shall examine in some detail in the rest of this chapter. These four periods are the Sensorimotor Period, beginning at birth and lasting 1½ to 2 years; the Preoperational Period, from 1½-2 to 6-7 years; the Concrete Operational Period, from 6-7 to 11-12 years; and the Formal Operational Period, from adolescence through adulthood. Table 2-1 summarizes these periods. Through-

TABLE 2-1

FOUR PERIODS OF COGNITIVE DEVELOPMENT

Period	*Approximate Age Ranges*
Sensorimotor	Birth—1½-2 years
Preoperational	1½-2—6-7 years
Concrete Operational	6-7—11-12 years
Formal Operational	11-12—through adulthood

out the book, ages associated with various periods and stages are meant to be rough approximations only. A brief discussion about the relation between age and stages of development can be found at the end of the chapter. In addition to describing stages and periods of general cognitive processes, Piaget described stages in the development of some specific abilities. While we shall be concerned primarily with the former, a brief description of one specific ability, recognition of object permanence, will be presented later in this chapter.

THE SENSORIMOTOR PERIOD

The first period of development is called *Sensorimotor* because the child solves problems using his sensory systems and motoric activity rather than the symbolic processes that characterize the other three major periods. The child's knowledge about objects comes from his actions on them. At this point we need to pause briefly to examine some perceptual-motor capabilities of the newborn. Then we shall return to Piaget's theory and see how the perceptual-motor system is used in the Sensorimotor Period.

Although the newborn infant may appear completely helpless at birth, many of his senses are functioning. From the moment of birth, when his eyes are open the newborn infant can see. The muscular control of eye movements is not very precise, and he has sharp focus only for those objects 9-10 inches from his face because the muscles controlling the curvature of the lenses are not fully developed. Nevertheless, the newborn can perceive color and shape when there is good contrast to the surrounding visual pattern. Since infants startle in response to loud noises and quiet in response to soft voices, we know that the sense of hearing functions from birth. Babies cry when stuck with a diaper pin and fuss when too hot or too cold; thus, we know that the senses of pain and temperature are operative. Touching, stroking, and rocking typically soothe a fussing infant, leading to the conclusion that the sense of touch and bodily posture cues are meaningful to the newborn. Finally, controlled experiments with a baby's reactions to different odors and tastes have permitted us to learn that the sense of smell works immediately from birth but taste discrimination is delayed for several days. Thus the infant is capable of receiving stimulation through the many sensory modalities he is born with.

In addition to perceiving stimulation, the newborn is capable of reflexive behavior. Reflexes are responses that all normal members of a species exhibit after a particular type of stimulation. Typically, psychologists consider reflexes unlearned. That is, the species-specific response occurs the very first time the stimulus is contacted, and it is not necessary for the organism to observe anyone else making that same response or to be taught. Examples of reflexes in adults are the knee-jerk when a doctor's hammer strikes the patella, and the constriction of the eye's pupil in response to bright light.

Some infant reflexes clearly have survival value. Among these are the rooting reflex, the sucking reflex, and the grasping reflex. The rooting reflex helps the infant locate his mother's breast for feeding. When a baby's cheek is stroked, he will turn his head toward the side that was touched and open his mouth. Then, when anything touches the infant's mouth, he begins sucking. Together the rooting and sucking reflexes ensure that, with a little help from his mother, the infant can obtain food. The grasping reflex is triggered by any object placed in the palm of the baby's hand. His grasp is strong enough that the infant just by grasping an adult's fingers can be pulled from a lying to a sitting position. The grasping reflex was probably significant in man's evolution when babies were transported by clinging to their mothers. Newborns also have reflexes for yawning, hiccoughing, sneezing, coughing, withdrawing an arm or leg if pricked with a pin, etc.

Other reflexes indicate how mature the infant is. The Babinski reflex, named after its discoverer, seems to be an indicator of the state of the central nervous system. When the outer sole of the infant's foot is stroked, the infant fans his toes apart and arches his foot. Between about 4 and 6 months of age, the Babinski reflex disappears and the infant now curls his toes downward in response to the sole stroke, just as adults do. If an infant still has a Babinski reflex after his first half year of life, damage to the central nervous system may be indicated.

Finally, there are reflexes whose functions are currently unknown. One example of this is the "walking" reflex. If an infant is held upright with his feet lightly touching a surface such as a table top, he will step in alternation, as if walking. These reflexes disappear, but the behaviors return later under voluntary control.

With the reflexes and sensory capacities outlined above, the infant is ready to begin interacting with his world. His reflexes allow his sensory systems to contact many objects. As he looks at, hears, touches, tastes, and smells things, he acquires valuable information about his environment. Before this interaction takes place, the infant does not know whether things are hot or cold, hard or soft, smooth or rough, sharp or blunt, tasty or ill-tasting. He does not even know what belongs to his body and what is part of the external world. He soon finds out, though, that biting his own toe causes pain whereas biting most other objects does not.

The amount of information an infant must learn is truly enormous and he has only his reflexes and sense organs with which to begin the process. The infant's reflexive systems are not as precise or discriminating as they could be.

Thus one of the first significant changes to occur is the modification of some of these reflexes. This takes place during the first of six stages within the Sensorimotor Period. We thus return to our discussion of Piaget's theory.

STAGE 1: MODIFICATION OF REFLEXES

When a child is born the sucking reflex is an automatic response to anything placed in the mouth. The reflex, at first, functions equally well to the stimulus of fingers or pieces of clothing as it does to nipples of bottles or breasts. During the first month of life, however, the sucking reflex becomes modified, enabling the hungry infant to suck more quickly and vigorously in response to milk while simultaneously enabling him to reject non-food substances. When he is no longer hungry the infant can reject food but will still suck on toys or pacifiers. The reflex thus becomes both more efficient and more voluntary. In other words, the infant learns to recognize objects by sucking on them and then can choose whether to suck or not.

In a similar manner the rooting reflex first becomes more efficient, turning the head in precisely the proper direction for a given stimulus, and then drops out as more voluntary movements replace the reflex. These voluntary head-turning movements arise from a combination of factors, including a maturing neuromuscular system and a conditioning process in which hunger, the presence of mother, and being held in a particular position are paired with the rooting and sucking reflexes.

Not all reflexes change in the Sensorimotor Period or, indeed, even in a person's lifetime. Thus pupil constriction to bright lights and withdrawal of a limb when pinpricked remain virtually unchanged. Nevertheless, those which do change demonstrate the significance of the first stage of the Sensorimotor Period.

STAGE 2: PRIMARY CIRCULAR REACTIONS

The second stage of the Sensorimotor Period has been called the stage of Primary Circular Reactions. During this time if the infant's random movements lead, by chance, to an interesting event, the infant will attempt to repeat the behavior. The term *circular reactions* refers to the circularity or repetitive aspects of the behavior. An example of a primary circular reaction might be thumb-sucking. The infant's thumb accidentally falls into his open mouth, triggering sucking, but then falls out. The infant then attempts to get his thumb back into his mouth so that the interesting event, sucking, can be repeated. The adjective "primary" refers to the fact that the interesting activity involves only the infant's own body. If there is any purpose to the circular reactions, it may be to practice the thumb-sucking scheme. Or, there may be no demonstrable purpose at all. In any case, there is no intention to suck the thumb to find out what the thumb is like. Such investigatory intent is hypothesized to occur only at later stages in the infant's development.

The Secondary Circular Reaction stage follows (logically enough) the Primary Circular Reaction stage. In this third stage of the Sensorimotor Period, the infant still exhibits circular reactions (repeating interesting chance occurring events), but now the repetitions involve events or objects in the external world, secondary to the infant's body. Piaget described an incident in which his son kicked his legs against his crib, thereby causing a toy suspended above the crib to swing. After observing a series of kicks followed by intense stares at the swinging toy, Piaget concluded that his son acted for the purpose of repeating an interesting event. It might be argued that the pleasure in seeing the swinging toy causes such excitement in the baby that his legs kicked, which accidentally resulted in the toy swinging again, which in turn excited the baby again to swing his legs, etc. Piaget rejected this explanation because he noticed that the rest of the baby's body did not become excited (arm movements dropped off) and the kicking became just precisely the movements needed to make the toy swing. The toy did not swing when the baby waved his feet in the air and these movements stopped. When his feet alternately hit the mattress, the toy did swing and these movements increased. If excitation from seeing the toy swing produced the kicking, there would be no reason for the kicking to become refined. Thus, intentionality can be inferred because of the refinements that occurred in the kicking.

Even though the infant in the Secondary Circular Reaction stage knows there is a connection between his behavior and the interesting event, the infant still has several cognitive deficiencies. His behavior is not fully intentional, in the sense that the goal was discovered by accident. It is only after the interesting event has occurred that the infant desires it. In addition, his behavior is aimed solely at reproducing the prior events; he is not yet inventing new behaviors.

STAGE 4: COORDINATION OF
SECONDARY REACTIONS

In Stage 4 the child can combine two or more previously acquired schemes to obtain a goal. The name of the stage is derived from this new achievement. The child coordinates several of his secondary circular reactions. One frequently cited example from Piaget's observations involved his child reaching for a matchbox Piaget was holding. Piaget held a pillow in one hand, in front of his other hand which held the matchbox, thus presenting an obstacle in front of a goal. He observed his child strike the pillow to displace it and clear the way to grab the matchbox. By putting the previously acquired pillow-striking and matchbox-grabbing schemes together in a coordinated manner, an object was overcome and the goal was reached. In earlier stages, the child might have given up his attempts to grab the matchbox as soon as an obstacle was imposed, or he might have been distracted into striking the pillow repeatedly. What is new about this stage is the child's continued orientation toward a specific goal. In the sense that only previous behaviors are joined together, however, there is no novelty. That accomplishment comes in the next stage of development.

STAGE 5: TERTIARY CIRCULAR REACTIONS

The Tertiary Circular Reaction stage is the fifth stage in the Sensorimotor Period. As the term "circular reactions" implies, events are still repeated, but the child has progressed to the point of actively seeking novelty. Actions are no longer repeated in exactly the same manner from trial to trial as was done in earlier stages. Now the child purposely varies his movements to observe the results. Actions are performed as if the infant were learning about the properties of objects as objects or actions as actions, not merely acting to obtain some goal. This involves novelty for its own sake, but the novel actions still develop by trial and error. The child does not know the outcome of his behavior until he tries it.

To clarify the distinction between the stages of secondary and tertiary circular reactions, consider a child in his playpen with a variety of toys. A secondary circular reaction might involve the child dropping a block from shoulder height and watching it bounce off the floor. In repeating the action, the child would continue with the same block and always release it from shoulder level. In the Tertiary Circular Reaction stage the child might vary the height of his release, from his head to just barely above the floor. He might vary what he dropped, trying out all the toys available. Or, he might vary both the height and the toy simultaneously.*

* Parents are urged to be patient if their child, playing this dropping game, happens to pitch the toys out of the playpen. After all, what are parents for, if not to retrieve the toys so that baby can drop them again. Parents also should not be surprised when peas and meat are dropped from the highchair. It is just a way of learning how these objects behave, although it is more likely that baby will learn how parents behave.

STAGE 6: BEGINNING OF
REPRESENTATIONAL THOUGHT

Stage 6 is the beginning of representational thought. Before this stage, the child could solve problems, learning
how to act deliberately and efficiently to achieve a desired
goal. But, Piaget stated that a child does not start to *think
without acting* before entering the sixth stage of the Sensorimotor Period. Representational thinking, according to
Piaget, involves mentally reasoning about a problem *prior*
to acting. A child tries to solve problems using his familiar
schemes, but if these fail, he will not grope around in the
trial-and-error fashion of prior stages. Rather, now the child
will consider the situation mentally, perhaps drawing an
analogy from a different time and place, and then directly
act on the problem with a scheme never before applied to
it. Piaget described his daughter's attempts to remove a
chain from a matchbox which was too nearly closed for
her to insert her hand and grasp the chain. According to
Piaget, many times before she had grasped the chain, but
she had always been able to insert her hand through the
opening. She first applied an old scheme, pushing her fingers into the box, but that did not work. In earlier stages of
development she might have applied other schemes such
as shaking the box or biting it. Now Piaget observed her to
open and close her mouth a little bit, then open it a bit
wider and then still wider. Finally she put a finger into the
opening of the matchbox, pulled it wider, and grasped the
chain. Piaget believed she solved the problem by examin-
ing her old schemes mentally, rather than by trying each of
them overtly. Reasoning by the analogy with opening her
mouth wider, she invented a novel solution to her problem.
Piaget did not believe that the Sensorimotor child's
thought involved language because the child's language

development was still too rudimentary in this stage. As the child first learns to speak, word meanings are unstable and idiosyncratic. The child does not realize that the meaning of a word must be agreed upon by the language community, so he changes the meaning to suit his own purposes. For example, a child might use the syllable "mu" to represent first his milk, then a cookie, his dog, and finally his mother, all within the span of a few hours. By the end of the Sensorimotor Period, the child is using only one, or

TABLE 2-2

SIX STAGES OF THE SENSORIMOTOR PERIOD

Stage	Principal Characteristics
1. Modification of Reflexes (0-1 month)	Reflexes become efficient and more voluntary movements replace them
2. Primary Circular Reactions (1-4 months)	Repetition of interesting body movements
3. Secondary Circular Reactions (4-10 months)	Repetition of interesting external events
4. Coordination of Secondary Reactions (10-12 months)	Combining schemes to obtain a goal
5. Tertiary Circular Reactions (12-18 months)	Varying repetition for novelty
6. Beginning of Representational Thought (18-24 months)	Thinking prior to acting

perhaps two, word utterances to label objects and express simple desires. While the meaning of a word is stable, the name is seen as such an integral part of the object that changing the name changes the object. Language usage is thus not developed enough to be useful for the new skill of representational thinking.

The six Sensorimotor stages span the child's development from the early reflexive behavioral responses, to repetitions of various activities involving the child's own body and other objects, to the beginning of mental reasoning prior to acting. (See Table 2-2 for an outline of the stages.) The child in the Sensorimotor Period uses his behavioral schemes to manipulate objects, to learn some of the properties of objects, and to obtain goals by combining several schemes. His behavior is tied to the concrete and the immediate, and he can only apply his schemes to objects he can perceive directly.

We have, thus far, traced Piaget's description of the six stages in the Sensorimotor Period. His descriptions arose from naturalistic observations he conducted on his own three children. Not much experimental research has been generated from this part of Piaget's theory, probably for a variety of reasons including the difficulty in working with subjects less than two years of age. Before describing the other major periods of development, we shall consider two specific abilities that develop during the Sensorimotor Period and which have been examined experimentally.

1. Object Permanence

Object permanence is defined as the knowledge that objects continue to exist even when one is not perceiving them. You know that this book continues to exist even if you put it on a shelf and leave the room. If it is not there when you return, you might start inquiring whether another person took it. Although the idea sometimes occurs to you, you do not really believe that it could "vanish into thin air." Does the child have this same knowledge of the permanence of objects from birth or is it something the child has to learn? Piaget suggested that object permanence is learned during the Sensorimotor Period in a series of stages* defined by the infant's searching behaviors.

According to Piaget, in the first stage (from birth to 2 months) the child will look at objects in his visual field, but if the objects leave his visual field he stops looking and

---

* The stages of object permanence development cut across the stages outlined above for the Sensorimotor Period. As a guide to the reader, approximate age ranges will be given here.

changes to some other activity. This results in the world being perceived as a series of fleeting images. Mother's face appears above the infant so he looks at her. If she steps away, he looks at other things.

The next stage (from 2 to 4 months) is characterized by "passive expectations." For a short while the infant will gaze at the location where the object disappeared, as if waiting for it to reappear. There is no active search, however, and Piaget does not credit the child with object permanence. He interprets the child's behavior as merely continuing an ongoing activity. Consider, for example, a child waving a rattle. If the rattle accidentally slips from the child's hand to the floor, the child will just continue waving his hand. He will not look around on the floor for the rattle.

TABLE 2-3

SIX STAGES IN THE ACQUISITION
OF OBJECT PERMANENCE

Approximate Ages	Principal Characteristics
1. 0-2 months	No expectations or searching
2. 2-4 months	Passive expectations
3. 4-8 months	Search for partially covered objects
4. 8-12 months	Search for completely covered objects
5. 12-18 months	Search after visible displacements
6. 18 + months	Search after hidden displacements

In the next stage (roughly 4 to 8 months) the child can anticipate the trajectory of the object and look for it at its landing place. This search is usually limited to looking for objects that the child himself has caused to disappear, but it shows what Piaget considered to be the beginnings of true object permanence. Also in this stage the child will reach for a partially covered object. If it disappears completely, though, he will stop reaching.

From about 8 to 12 months, the child will search for objects that other people have caused to disappear, but he cannot do so successfully (i.e., find the object) if a series of movements (displacements) has to be considered. Piaget's demonstration of this involved showing a child a toy and then placing the toy under a cover. The child in this stage immediately lifts the cover and obtains the toy. This sequence is repeated, and again the child finds the toy. On the third trial, however, the child watches as the toy is hidden in a different location, under a pillow. Once it disappears from sight, the child turns away and looks for it under the cover where it was hidden the first two times. Although the child apparently knows that the object exists, he confers a certain "privilege of position" on it and includes where an object can be found in the definition of the object.

By the beginning of the child's second year of life (12 to 18 months), he learns how to handle the displacements described above. He will search for the object where it was last seen. However, he has to see the displacements to be able to follow them. If the toy is hidden under the cover, the cover and toy are both put under the pillow, and then only the cover is removed, the child will not search for the toy under the pillow. Searching after hidden displacements occurs only after the final stage in the development of object permanence (18 months onward).

While Piaget's descriptions of the child's active search for objects is accurate, one can ask whether active search is the best response to use as an indication of object permanence. There is a recurrent suspicion in developmental psychology that the child may *know* something before he can demonstrate his knowledge because of lack of development in some related function. For example, the child might know an object has permanence before he can actively search for it because active search involves the development of eye-hand coordination—to reach exactly where one is looking. Or, the child might know an object exists but forget about the object due to a limited memory span. This latter hypothesis, in fact, was offered by T. G. R. Bower (1971) after he conducted an experiment on object permanence in young infants.

Bower's test of object permanence
Since Bower wanted to test very young infants, who would not reach for objects, he used a simple response, the surprise or startle reaction, as the potential indicator of object permanence. The babies in his experiment were either 20, 40, 80, or 100 days old, corresponding to infants in Piaget's first two stages in the development of object permanence. Bower propped each baby up in a sitting position so that the baby faced a brightly colored object, such as a ball. As the infant looked at the ball, a screen moved in front of it, hiding the ball from the infant's view. The screen remained in front of the ball for either $1^{1}/_{2}$, 3, $7^{1}/_{2}$, or 15 seconds. Then the screen moved away. On half of the trials the ball was visible again. On the other half of the trials the ball had disappeared. Bower reasoned that if the babies had a notion of object permanence, they should expect the ball to be visible when the screen moved off. Being visible again should produce no reaction, but if the ball had disappeared, the babies should be quite surprised. On the other hand, if the infants have no notion of object permanence, they should be surprised to see it and not surprised when it had disappeared. In this experiment surprise was measured by watching the babies' facial expressions. In other experiments more sophisticated measures of heart rate and breathing changes have indicated the same results. Figure 2-1 presents the alternative outcomes possible.

39

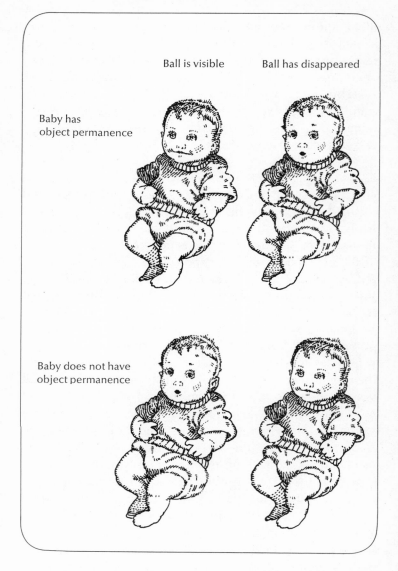

Figure 2-1. Possible reactions by babies with or without object permanence, depending on the conditions of the experiment.

The results of this little experiment depended upon the age of the baby and the length of time the screen hid the ball. All age groups of babies were surprised when the ball was gone if the screen had been in front for only 1½ seconds. None was surprised on the trials when the ball was still there. Together these two results indicate some object permanence by infants as young as 20 days. The oldest infants expected the object to be there even after the longest time interval. The youngest infants, however, were more surprised to see the ball remain than disappear at the longest time interval. That is, after 15 seconds of hiding, the youngest babies appeared not to have object permanence. (See Figure 2-2.) Apparently, then, 20-day-old babies will show some object permanence if the conditions are proper (only 1½ seconds of hiding), but lack of development in processes such as memory prevents the infant from having a fully developed conception of object permanence. A more refined and complete understanding of object permanence does have to be developed, and this is one of the major achievements of the Sensorimotor Period.

2. Object Recognition

A second major achievement of the Sensorimotor Period involves a change in the features an infant uses to recognize an object. As adults, we use an object's size, shape, color, texture, etc. to identify it. Do these same features help the infant recognize an object? Bower (1971) performed an experiment to answer this question.

The infants who served as subjects in this experiment were between 6 and 22 weeks of age. Each infant was seated facing a screen, and a railroad track ran from left to right, passing behind the screen. (See Figure 2-3.) Each baby was exposed to four different situations. In the first situation a small white mannikin was placed at the left end

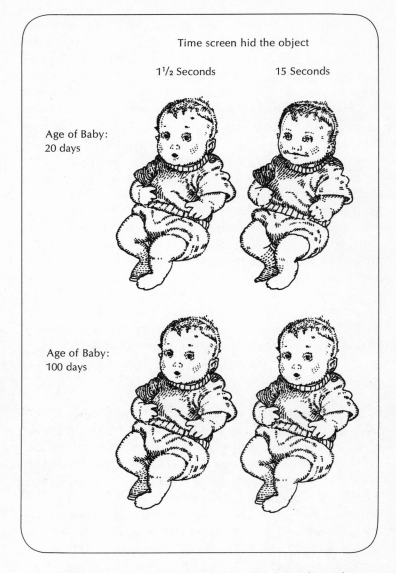

Time screen hid the object

1½ Seconds   15 Seconds

Age of Baby:
20 days

Age of Baby:
100 days

Figure 2-2. Surprise and nonsurprise reactions obtained on trials when the ball has disappeared in Bower's experiment on object permanence.

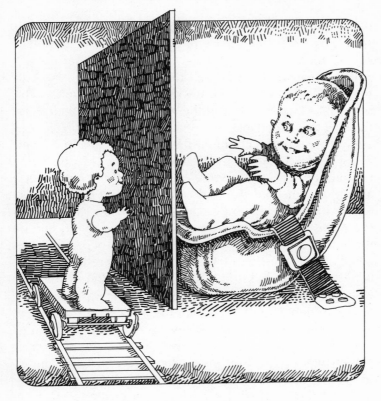

Figure 2-3. Location of baby, screen, and railroad track in Bower's experiment on object recognition.

of the track. It then moved along the track at a constant speed, passed behind the screen, emerged from the other side, stopping at the right end of the track. After a short pause the mannikin reversed directions, moving back to the original left end of the track, again passing behind the screen. All babies followed the movement with their eyes, tracking the mannikin.

In the second condition the white mannikin moved along the track and, at the time when it should have reappeared from behind the screen, an entirely different object, a red lion, emerged. The red lion traveled to the right end of the track, paused, moved back behind the screen, and the white mannikin reappeared, moving to the left end of the track. Seeing a difference in size, shape, and color, adults would conclude that two objects were being used. Babies over 16 weeks old followed the motion of the lion when it emerged, but there was some glancing back at the screen. When the lion paused at the right end of the track, there were definite looks at the screen about ¹/₄ of the time. This was taken as an indication that many of the babies knew that two objects had been involved. Babies under 16 weeks of age showed a very different pattern of responses. They tracked the moving object with no glancing back toward the screen.

In the third condition, the white mannikin moved toward the right and went behind the screen. According to its speed of movement, the object should be behind the screen for a certain length of time. In this condition, a white mannikin emerged "too fast." That is, just after the first white mannikin disappeared behind the screen, an identical one emerged from the other side. As in the other conditions the entire sequence was repeated in reverse. Adults will take this as an indication of two different but identical-looking objects. All the babies over 16 weeks looked back at the screen after the one object had stopped, apparently waiting for the second object to emerge. Babies under 16 weeks got very upset and refused to look anymore. They did not track the movement of the object that emerged.

The fourth condition was a combination of the previous two. As the white mannikin moved toward the right and passed behind the screen, a red lion emerged "too fast." When the red lion reversed directions and moved behind the screen, the white mannikin emerged "too fast." The reactions to this condition were similar to the third condition. Babies over 16 weeks looked back at the screen after they had tracked the emerging object. Babies under 16 weeks cried and refused to look. Table 2-4 summarizes these results.

Bower concluded that younger infants are not affected by feature differences as are older children and adults. Rather, they respond to changes in the speed of a moving object. From the ages tested in this experiment, it appears that features like size, shape, and color come to control the identification of objects somewhere around 16 weeks of age. It is important to remember that infants can *perceive* size, shape, and color differences. Bower's experiment just suggests that before 16 weeks infants do not use the information about size, shape, and color to make decisions about the *identity* of objects. How the transition is made from the younger infants' reliance on speed of movement to the older infants' use of feature components is unclear at the present time. Bower's research on object identification did not stem from a consideration of Piagetian concepts as did his research on object permanence. Nevertheless, both studies demonstrate important changes that occur in infants during the Sensorimotor Period.

The child from two to six years has been studied more than the infant, especially the four-to-five-year-olds who attend nursery school. So let us now turn to this age child and the second major period of cognitive development, the Preoperational Period.

Table 2-4

Results of Bower's Experiment on Object Recognition

| Condition | | Age of Babies | |
Objects	Speed	Under 16 weeks	Over 16 weeks
1. Mannikin	Normal	Track moving object	Track moving object
2. Mannikin→Lion	Normal	Track moving object	Track moving object and some glances at screen
3. Mannikin	Too Fast	Refuse to look	Track moving object and look back at screen
4. Mannikin→Lion	Too Fast	Refuse to look	Track moving object and look back at screen

THE PREOPERATIONAL PERIOD

The distinguishing characteristic of the Preoperational child is the development of "symbolic functioning." Symbolic functioning is the ability to make one thing represent a different thing which is not present. The degree of correspondence between the two can vary from highly concrete to highly abstract. That is, if one uses a toy hammer made of plastic to represent a real metal hammer, the degree of correspondence is highly concrete. A mental picture or image of a hammer is more abstract but may retain some features of the thing represented, such as color and shape. The word made up of the letters *h, a, m, m, e, r* is a highly abstract symbol for the real object, printed letters on a page bearing only an arbitrary relationship to the metal tool. Piaget argued that the acquisition of symbolic functions enables the child to increase his sphere of activity to include past and future events as well as present ones. That is, he can apply his schemes to nonimmediate events. This use of symbolic functions is one of the major distinctions between a child in the Preoperational Period and one in the Sensorimotor Period.

Symbolic functions have been inferred from four types of activities of the Preoperational child: search for hidden objects, delayed imitation, symbolic play, and language. Having acquired object permanence, as discussed earlier, the Preoperational child can follow hidden displacements. In order to guide his own searching behavior, the child must have some sort of mental representation of the hidden object and of the unseen movements of displacement. At younger ages when the child would only search if he perceived the object, the perception of the object could be said to guide his search. Now some kind of symbolic function must take over the guidance.

Delayed imitation is, as the name implies, imitation of a behavior some time after the behavior was observed. It is postulated that as the child observes the model, he forms an internal representation of the behavior. Later the recall of this internal representation controls imitation. Piaget rejected the idea that language was the primary mode of internal representation used in delayed imitation and search for hidden objects because the behaviors displayed are much too complex for the child to describe verbally. He cited the example of his daughter, who one day watched a playmate throw a temper tantrum, stamping his feet and howling. The next day Piaget's daughter stood up in her playpen, stamped her feet and howled just as she had seen the friend do the day before. Her actions had a deliberateness about them which suggested that she was trying out a new behavior, to see what it was like. Without a symbolic means of learning and then recalling the temper tantrum actions, his daughter could not have imitated them a day later.

In symbolic play the child treats an object as if it were

something else. This is readily seen in the child's use of a broomstick as a plane, a doll as a friend, fingers as guns, etc. One object is made to stand for another in the make-believe world of play.

In the Preoperational Period language begins to be used symbolically, as the child describes activities of the past and understands some references to the future. His use of words is more conventional (though by no means perfectly adult-like) and comes to control more of his behavior. One function of language is to teach the child how to organize or classify his environment. If two objects are both given the name, "chair," then the child learns that they belong together in some sense. That is, the child can guess that any new object given the name "chair" is good for sitting on. Similarly, he soon learns that any strange offering called "candy" will probably taste good. The Preoperational child thus begins to learn about the formal properties of classes.

Classes are, in essence, the categories into which we divide objects. These class divisions are made along one or more dimensions (or properties) of the objects. For example, one can classify objects according to their shapes, resulting in the class of square objects, the class of circular objects, the class of triangular objects, etc. Or, one can classify objects according to their color, resulting in the classes of red things, blue things, green things, and yellow things. One of the properties of classes, according to Piaget, is that no object may belong to two classes *along the same dimension* simultaneously. Thus a large blue square could, if classification were according to shape, belong to the class of square things, but it could not simultaneously belong to a class of circular things or triangular things. It could, however, also belong to another class based on a different dimension such as color. In other words, classes along one dimension are mutually exclusive, but classes along independent dimensions may overlap.

All objects in one class have some common trait. A large blue square and a small red square share squareness. This property, squareness, gives the class its definition and is what Piaget has called *intension*. Circularity is the intension of a class of circles. Blueness is the intension, the defining characteristic, of the class of blue objects.

A class can also be described by listing its members. This has been called the *extension* of the class. The extension of a class of flowers could be roses, tulips, pansies, daisies, etc. Finally, the *intension* of a class determines its *extension*. If the intension of a class is "fully enclosed, stationary structures in which people live," the extension of the class must include tents, teepees, houses, cottages, and hotels.

During the Preoperational Period the child comes to know some of the basic properties of classes. He demonstrates this knowledge by sorting objects according to the various classes they belong to. The typical task, called the multiple classification problem, is to present the child with an array of cards such as pink and yellow, large and small, circles and squares. The child with a firm understanding of class properties can sort the cards into two groups in three separate ways, according to each of the three dimensions, color, size, and shape. A child who does not yet have a firm understanding of classes will show any of several common mistakes. The first mistake to appear is forming a picture out of the cards. The child might not know what is being asked of him, he might think the task is too difficult, or he might simply decide not to cooperate. Frosty the Snowman was the product of one child asked to sort cards. (See Figure 2-4a.) The second error to appear is to change the basis of the groupings several times. The child may start out putting all pink things together, so he places two pink small circles next to each other, then a pink small square, then he changes the dimension of the sort to shape and puts a large yellow square next, followed by a small yellow square. (See Figure 2-4b.) There appears to be no single intension, or defining property, regulating the sorting. The third mistake is to sort according to all dimensions simultaneously, ignoring the instructions to form only two piles. For example, the child may form discrete groups of small yellow circles, small pink circles, large yellow squares, etc. Classes, for this type of child, are only identical objects rather than any other object sharing a trait. (See Figure 2-4c.)

By the end of the Preoperational Period children demon-

Figure 2-4. Typical sorting errors on a multiple classification task.

a. "Frosty the Snowman" created by a child who ignored the instructions to sort the cards into two piles.
b. This arrangement was created by a child who changed dimensions from pink to square for one of the two piles.
c. This arrangement was created by a child who formed discrete piles of identical objects.

strate a basic understanding of classes. When asked to sort cards, they will choose one dimension (e.g., size) to serve as the basis for the sort. All objects having a certain value along the dimension (e.g., the intension, large) will be placed together while those objects having another value along the same dimension (e.g., the intension, small) will be amassed. Moreover, no objects will be left out of the sort.

Thus we have seen that two of the major accomplishments of the Preoperational Period are the use of symbolic functions and the beginnings of an understanding of classes. Despite these accomplishments, the Preoperational child's thinking is still severely limited. Piaget asserted that the Preoperational child is unable to focus his attention on two different dimensions of a problem simultaneously. The Preoperational child exhibits *centration,* the focusing of attention on only one aspect of a situation, when *decentration* is required to reach a solution. Centration shows up in three tasks concerning ordinal relations, in tests comparing parts to wholes (called the class inclusion problem), and in conservation problems.

The ordinal relations problem asks the child to put elements in a series according to one quantifiable dimension. That is, the task is to arrange objects in some order, *relative to each other*. For example, the child is given a series of sticks of increasing length and told to arrange them from shortest to longest. A Preoperational child might proceed as follows: he takes two sticks from the main pile, compares them, and puts the shorter of the two on his left. Then he takes another stick from the pile and compares it

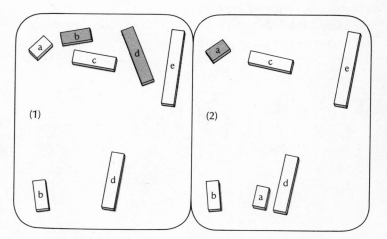

Figure 2-5. Typical sorting error of sticks according to their lengths.

(1) Two sticks (b and d) are randomly selected from the pile and compared. The shorter is placed to the left.
(2) One of the remaining sticks (a) is randomly selected from the pile, compared to one of the previously sorted sticks (d), and placed to the left of (d) since it is shorter. No comparison is made between sticks (a) and (b).

with only one of the two prior sticks. If it is shorter, it gets placed on the left without regard for its length relative to the other original stick. (See Figure 2-5.) Piaget's explanation for the Preoperational child's behavior is that he can focus on only one aspect of the problem at a time. In this case the child focuses on one paired comparison at a time rather than on the total array. An older child might solve this problem by scanning the main pile, removing the shortest stick, scanning the pile again and removing what is then the shortest stick, etc. Each time he considers the entire problem as well as the arrangement he is forming.

PART–WHOLE (CLASS INCLUSION)

The part–whole problem also gives the Preoperational child difficulties. In the most common task, the child is shown 7 blue beads and 3 white beads, all made of wood. He is asked if there are more blue beads or more wood beads. Because the Preoperational child cannot focus his attention both on the parts (white and blue) and on the whole (wood) simultaneously, he errs in his judgment. The following is an interchange between a five-year-old boy and an adult.

Adult: Do you see all these beads I have? Some of them are blue and some are white. What do you think the blue beads are made of?
Child: Wood.
Adult: That's right. And what do you think the white ones are made of?
Child: Wood.
Adult: Good. Both the blue beads and the white beads are made of wood. Now I have a question for you. Do you think there are more blue beads or wood beads?
Child: Blue.
Adult: Why?
Child: Because there are more.
Adult: More what?
Child: More blue.
Adult: More blue than what?
Child: More blue than white.
    Thinking that the child might have misheard the question, more directive questions were attempted.
Adult: But I wanted to know about the wooden beads. Are the white beads made out of wood?
Child: Yes.

Adult: Are the blue beads made out of wood?
Child: Yes.
Adult: So all the beads are made out of wood?
Child: Yes.
Adult: So are there more *wood* beads or blue beads?
Child: Blue.

The child is not really being stubborn. He is just unable to make comparisons across two levels of a hierarchy of classes. In other words, he does not realize that the two classes formed on the basis of color (white and blue) can be combined to form a larger single class based on material (wood). Piaget maintained that the child would have to focus on two aspects of a task (both the higher unified class and one of the lower classes) at the same time to be able to solve the class inclusion problem. Such an ability is characteristic of a child in the next major period of development, the Concrete Operational Period.

The child's failure on the class inclusion problem has occasionally been attributed to the particular question asked, i.e., "Are there more blue beads or wood beads?" Changing the question, however, has not resulted in improved performance. One variation is to tell the child that the examiner wants to make a necklace of all the wood beads, then changes his mind and wants a necklace of blue beads. Then the child is asked which necklace would be longer, the wood one or the blue one. A child in the Preoperational Period firmly insists on the blue necklace.

In addition to his difficulty with the class inclusion and ordinal relation problems, the Preoperational child does not succeed in conservation tasks. In any of the various conservation tasks, the child watches the tester change some features of an object and must decide that some other features do not change. For example, if two quantities are equal along one dimension, such as number, but appear to be unequal along another dimension, such as length or density, the Preoperational child will be mistaken in his judgment concerning the numerical equality. The task can be presented as follows: On a table between the child and the tester a row of 5 red checkers is placed. Below the 5 red checkers are placed 5 black checkers, aligned so that each black checker is directly below a red one. (See Figure 2-6a.) The child is asked if the two rows have the same number of checkers, or if the red row has more, or if the black row has more. Children above about the ages of three or four will say that the rows have the same number. As the child watches, the black row is spread out (see Figure 2-6b) until the arrangement seen in Figure 2-6c is created. Then the child is again asked if the two rows have the same number of checkers or if one has more than the other. Children in the Preoperational Period reply either that the black row has more "because it is longer" or that the red row has more "because they are all bunched up" (i.e., more dense). In contrast, children in the Concrete Operational Period will correctly reply that the numbers have stayed the same, recognizing that perceptual changes in length or density have no effect on numerical quantity.

To make sure that the idea of conservation of number had generality and was not restricted to rows of checkers,

Figure 2-6. A conservation of number task with checkers.

a. The starting arrangement from the child's point of view.
b. The experimenter spreads out one row.
c. The ending arrangement from the child's point of view.

Figure 2-7. A conservation of number task with cars.

a. The starting arrangement
b. The child places a car in each container simultaneously
c. The ending arrangement

Piaget devised several different conservation of number tasks. In one of them, the child is given a pile of 10 cars and shown two jars. One jar is tall and thin; the other is short and wide. The child is instructed to take a car in each hand and drop each car in the jar in front of his hand at the same time. After doing this five times, of course, there are 5 cars in each jar, but the tall thin jar appears to be full while the short wide one is not. (See Figure 2-7.)

The child is then asked if each jar has the same number of cars. A Preoperational child who does not conserve number either points to the tall thin jar as having more, because it is taller or because it is "all filled up," or he points to the short wide jar, saying it has more because "it's fatter."

In summary, we have seen that the Preoperational child uses symbolic functions and begins to understand classes but he fails to compare parts to wholes (in the class inclusion problem), does not order serial quantities well (ordinal relations problem), and does not conserve number. Piaget attributes these limitations in thinking to the child's inability to decenter his attention.

THE CONCRETE OPERATIONAL PERIOD

In contrast to the Preoperational child, the Concrete Operational child can solve a variety of tasks. When asked whether there are more blue beads or wood beads, the Concrete Operational child can state that there are more wood beads. He can place sticks in a series by length, and he can conserve number.

Typical of Piaget's approach to psychological investigation, he believed that the reasons or justifications for a child's response was important. He found that in the conservation of number task three types of reasons for conservation responses were offered. The *counting* justification proves two rows equal by counting each row. A *one-to-one correspondence* response reflects the idea that for every checker in the red row, there is a corresponding checker in the black row. In the *associativity* response the child states that rearranging the parts does not affect the whole. To put it in the words of an eight-year-old, "All you did was spreaded* them out."

Why does the Concrete Operational child succeed in the conservation of number task when the Preoperational

* A discussion of children's use of past tense verbs is beyond the scope of this book.

child fails? Piaget suggested that the Concrete Operational child has acquired three mental processes, called *operations,* which guide his thinking.

One operation is *negation.* Compressing a row of checkers can be negated by its opposite—spreading them out again. In the Preoperational Period, the child tends to focus on the beginning state (the apparent equality of the rows) and the end state (the perceptual inequality) and ignores the intervening activity. That is, he ignores the process of transformation. The Concrete Operational child can attend to the process (the compressing or spreading out) and thus learns that one action negates or reverses the other.

The second operation is *reciprocation.* The child sees that one row has increased in length but decreased in density compared with the other row. Since length and density are reciprocal features, a change in length compensates for a change in density, resulting in no net change to the object. Although the operations of reciprocation and negation are similar, they can be distinguished from each other. In using negation, the Concrete Operational child attends to the process of transformation. In using reciprocation, the child attends to the multiple features of the end state, both length and density, and recognizes the reciprocal relationship between them.

The third mental operation, called *identity,* can also be used by the Concrete Operational child to conserve number. When the child realizes that nothing has been added or removed, he knows that number remains the same.

As with each new cognitive skill the child acquires, it takes practice to apply that skill correctly and efficiently to new problems. The Concrete Operational child, having mastered conservation of number, must also master conservation of other dimensions such as liquid quantity, mass, and length. The liquid quantity conservation task is very

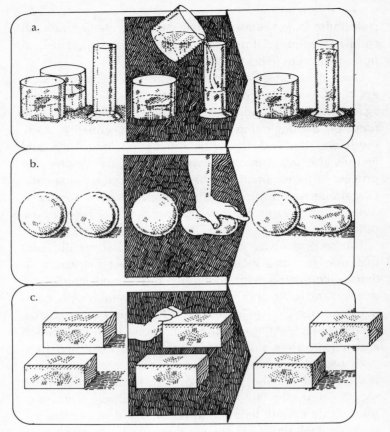

Figure 2-8. Conservation of liquid, mass, and length tasks.

a. Conservation of liquid
b. Conservation of mass
c. Conservation of length

similar to the conservation of number task described above. The child is shown two identical beakers filled with identical amounts of colored water. The child judges the beakers to have equal amounts. Then, as the child watches, the liquid is poured from one of the original beakers into a taller, thinner beaker. Then he is asked to compare the newly filled beaker with the other original one. (See Figure 2-8a.) An alternative task for the conservation of liquid quantity involves pouring liquid from one of the original beakers into five much smaller containers. The nonconserving child will either indicate that the original beaker has more because it is taller or that the five small containers have more because there are five of them. The classical problem for conservation of mass presents the child with two clay balls. Then one is either rolled into a sausage or flattened like a pancake. (See Figure 2-8b.) To conserve, the child needs to recognize that changes in shape do not indicate changes in mass. In the conservation of length task, the child must judge that length stays the same even though position has shifted. (See Figure 2-8c.) In all there are approximately ten different conservation tasks which test for the recognition of preservation of equality in the face of compelling changes in spatial arrangement.

Piaget's description and explanation of conservation prompted research aimed at two related questions: (1) Could children be easily trained to conserve several years before they normally develop the ability? and (2) Was the development of operations the proper explanation for children's classification and conservation responses?

The initial attempts to teach conservation involved demonstrating to the subjects the logical operations such as reciprocation, negation, and identity. For example, a child might be shown how to weigh a ball of clay, then that changing the shape did not change the weight, and that adding more clay and then removing the same amount left the weight unchanged (Smedslund, 1960). Basically, these studies met with little success. The children did not show conservation on the tests after training, and it was tentatively concluded that children had to be biologically more mature to profit from the experience.

The next attempts at training taught subskills which could be relevant to conservation. Kingsley and Hall (1967), for example, trained conservation of length to five- and six-year-olds by teaching five subskills: (1) what the terms *longer* and *shorter* meant; (2) how to measure with an independent device (ruler); (3) that the ruler was more reliable than visual cues; (4) that length was changed only when quantity is added or subtracted from the ends; and (5) that moving an object did not change its length.

Since conservation of length was indeed learned by the children, it appeared that the answer to the question, can children be taught conservation, was "yes," but with the qualifying statement that it is not as easy to teach as might be supposed. This research shed no light, however, on the other question regarding the importance of logical operations in conservation. The failure to conserve after teaching logical operations directly was not seen as encouraging, so other explanations for conservation were sought.

One explanation which seemed worthy of investigation was that a young child might conserve if his attention were not so attracted to highly salient but irrelevant perceptual cues such as height, width, size, shape, color, etc. In the conservation of liquid quantity, the child is faced with two identical beakers containing equal amounts of water. From the child's point of view, quantity is a multi-dimensional concept and decisions might be reached on the basis of any one of several salient dimensions: height, width, shape, size, water level, or actual amount. From the experimenter's point of view, only the last, actual amount, is a relevant dimension. Often equality of amount coincides with equality on the other dimensions, so the child must learn which of the dimensions to attend to. Furthermore, when the liquid is poured to the new beaker, all of the dimensions *except* actual amount are changed. It is well known that changing a dimension is one way to attract attention to it. It is likely, therefore, that the younger child will attend to one of the irrelevant cues. If his attention is misdirected, then that will mask any attempts to find out whether he has logical operations such as addition, subtraction, reciprocation, etc.

In a study by Gelman (1969), a method was devised to train children to attend and respond to actual amount and to ignore the other, irrelevant cues. The subjects were children in kindergarten, about five years old. These children were chosen because they had failed to conserve on each of four conservation tasks (mass, liquid, number, and length) in the pretest (the test before training). Figure 2-9 shows the tasks used in the pretest.

Training took place on two consecutive days, with eight sets of problems on length and eight sets on number each

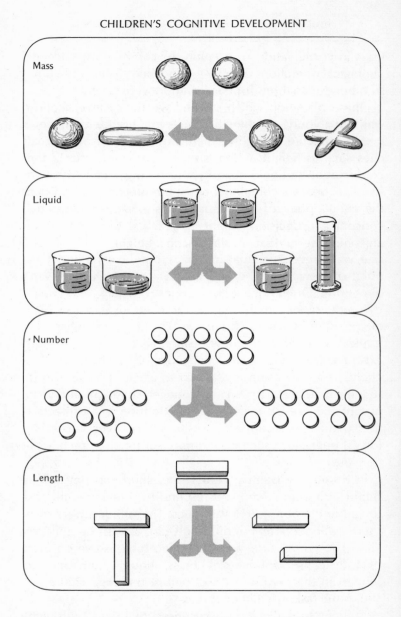

Figure 2-9. Conservation tasks used for the pretest in Gelman's experiment.

day. In each training trial, the child was confronted with three stimuli, two of which were identical and one was different. For example, there might be two 6-inch sticks and one 10-inch stick. On half the trials the child was asked to point to two things that were the same; on the other half of the trials the child was asked to point to two things which were different. The trials were arranged so as to reduce progressively the number of irrelevant cues which the child could use to make a correct response. On the first trial of a set all cues indicated the correct response. For example, in the length problem, the two identical sticks would be placed horizontally, in parallel, with ends aligned, while the third stick might be slightly vertical with neither end aligned. On trials 2-5, various placements would make the child choose incorrectly if he used some of the irrelevant cues. On the sixth trial none of the irrelevant cues suggested a correct response, for example, the three sticks would be spatially separated, non-parallel, with no ends aligned. If the child answered correctly, it could only be on the basis of the relevant cue, actual length.* Figure 2-10 gives an example of the six trials per set for a length task.

Two groups of children received identical experiences with the training stimuli with the one exception of whether or not they received feedback. In the experimental group, if the subject chose correctly, he was told he was correct and given a small trinket; if the subject chose incorrectly, he was told he was wrong and the next problem was presented. Subjects in the control group did not receive feedback after a trial. At the end of each session, they were merely told that they had played well.

All children were given two more conservation tests, one test on the day following training (the immediate post-test)

---

* This same procedure, called fading, can be used to teach many different kinds of discriminations between stimuli.

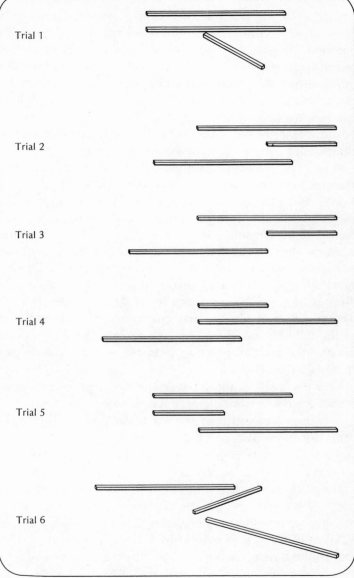

Figure 2-10. Examples of six trials for training conservation of length in Gelman's experiment.

and one test two to three weeks later (delayed post-test). These post-tests were comparable to the pretest and did not involve feedback. Figure 2-11 shows the percentages of correct responses by the two groups of children for the four conservation tasks. On the length and number tasks, for which there had been training, the experimental group got nearly perfect scores whereas the control group got only $1/4$ to $1/3$ correct. As Kingsley and Hall had previously shown, conservation can be taught to children a few years before it typically occurs. Gelman's study also clearly showed that the experimental group improved on other conservation tasks as well (mass and liquid), even though these had not been trained. Gelman concluded that two factors were important for training. First, children need an opportunity to work with many different arrangements of materials. This is what the control group did, and some specific learning seemed to occur. The second important factor is feedback which indicates to the child which definition of quantity to use. In other words, they need information about which dimension is relevant. With both feedback and opportunity, the experimental group learned a considerable amount about conservation tasks which were like the tasks on which they had been trained (length and number) and they transferred this knowledge to two other conservation tasks (mass and liquid quantity). Gelman's experiment demonstrated that some children do not give correct conservation responses because their attention is drawn to irrelevant aspects of the task. It appears that young children have a broad definition of the concept of quantity and need to learn to restrict the meaning to actual amount. How children acquire the broad meaning of quantity, how they naturally learn to restrict it, and when (or if) they learn logical operations remain unanswered questions.

The accomplishments of the Concrete Operational child

Figure 2-11. Average percentage of correct responses in Gelman's experiment

| | Immediate Post-test | | | |
	Length	Number	Mass	Liquid
Feedback during Training (Experimental Group)	95%	96%	58%	55%
No Feedback during Training (Control Group)	27%	21%	9%	4%

| | Delayed Post-test | | | |
	Length	Number	Mass	Liquid
Feedback during Training (Experimental Group)	90%	96%	65%	71%
No Feedback during Training (Control Group)	31%	29%	14%	3%

are outstanding, especially in comparison with the non-conserving Preoperational child. There are, however, limitations to the Concrete Operational child's problem-solving skills. As implied by the term "concrete," the Concrete Operational child applies his mental operations solely to real (concrete) objects or events. One can ask the child to consider the following question: If all dogs were pink and I had a dog, would it be pink too? The Concrete Operational child will balk at such a question, rejecting the initial supposition by stating that dogs cannot be pink. The Concrete Operational child cannot divorce himself from the objective world and think about purely hypothetical propositions. The Formal Operational child, in the last major period of cognitive development, can.

THE FORMAL OPERATIONAL PERIOD

The child (or adolescent) in the Formal Operational Period can construct contrary-to-fact hypotheses ("if dogs are pink") and reason about them. Once the child appreciates the fact that hypothetical problems can be solved by applying the same rules as would be applied to concrete problems, it follows that he will begin to consider many problems of the same type as belonging to the same class. The class of problems can then be solved by applying a rule which is abstract enough to cover all the specific instances. In other words, one facet of Formal Operational thinking is to organize single operations into higher order operations. This has also been referred to as "operating on operations" in contrast to operating directly on objects as the Concrete Operational child can do. The simplest example comes from mathematics. Given a problem such as "what number plus twenty equals twice itself?" the Concrete Operational child will use the operations of addition and multiplication on various numbers in a trial-and-error way. He might, for example, think of the number 5, insert it in the formula $(5 + 20 = 25 \rightarrow 2 \times 5 = 10)$, and decide it was incorrect. He would continue to try numbers in this manner until he found the correct one. The Formal Operational child will develop an abstract rule, $x + 20 = 2x$, and solve the formula algebraically, $20 = 2x - x = x$. The separate operations of addition and multiplication would be combined into a higher-order algebraic operation.

With the new ability to consider hypothetical, abstract problems the adolescent in the Formal Operational Period is led to consider his own beliefs and thoughts as valid objects of inquiry. Thinking becomes just as much a subject to be reasoned about as other, more concrete problems. Mussen, Conger, and Kagan (1974) report an adolescent who said, "I find myself thinking about my future and then I began to think about why I was thinking about my future and then I began to think about why I was thinking about why I was thinking about my future" (p. 314).

Another notable aspect of Formal Operational thinking is the systematic checking of all possible alternative solutions to a problem. When confronted with a problem, the Concrete Operational child is likely to come up with one solution, and, if it sounds at all reasonable, he will stop. The Formal Operational child will generate multiple alternatives and examine each of them. For example, if a child were asked why a man was lying in the middle of the sidewalk, the Concrete Operational child might propose that the man was drunk and fell down. The Formal Operational child will consider that the man may be drunk, or had a heart attack, or was hit on the head by a robber, or is playing a joke, etc. The Formal Operational child, thus, thinks about all logically possible alternative solutions in a systematic fashion. He uses his knowledge about the different possible solutions to guide his behavior. To demonstrate this in an experimental setting, a type of chemistry problem can be presented. The child is shown five colorless, odorless liquids in test-tubes and told to discover what combination of the five will produce a yellow mixture. The Concrete Operational child attempts to solve this problem through trial-and-error. He merely starts combining liquids. But, without an overall plan of action, one which is systematic, he soon becomes hopelessly lost—not remembering which combinations he has already tried and which he has left to try. The Formal Operational child proceeds in a more systematic fashion such as combining the first and second test-tubes, then the first and third, then the first and fourth, first and fifth, second and third, etc. until the solution is found.

A third major feature of the Formal Operational Period is that many different aspects of a problem can be dealt with simultaneously. The Concrete Operational child thinks sequentially, considering only one aspect of a problem at a time. As soon as several aspects can be considered together, in the Formal Operational Period, the logic of a *set* of beliefs can be examined.* The adolescent is likely to consider his own beliefs, about religion, politics, morality, education, etc., in terms of their logical consistency. Kagan (1971 a) provides the following example:

(1). *God loves man.*
(2). *The world contains many unhappy people.*
(3). *If God loved man, he would not make so many people unhappy. [p. 1001]*

While the adolescent might resolve the inconsistency among these three statements by supposing that man is made unhappy for some ulterior motive, current American adolescents tend to resolve the contradictions by denying the existence of God. Once he does that, all of his beliefs become suspect and fair game for further attack. The

---

* Just because a person has the capacity to examine his own sets of beliefs does not mean that he always does so. This might explain why one's own children commit only harmless pranks while the neighborhood urchins engage in malicious mischief.

adolescent is likely to challenge the adults around him to explain the inconsistencies he has found in a variety of previously accepted ideas. One can readily see where the image of an argumentative and rebellious youth comes from.

GENERAL ISSUES

RESEARCH STRATEGIES

The first wave of research generated by Piaget's writings was aimed primarily at confirming (or disconfirming) his descriptions of the various stages and periods of development. It is probable that so much energy was spent in replicative research because Piaget's methodology appeared weak in contrast to traditional American research. In brief, Piaget's approach is a flexible questioning procedure, permitting the tester to rephrase questions that the child did not understand and encouraging the child to expand brief verbal responses. The latter in particular is a delicate procedure because the tester must be careful not to suggest answers to the child. At the same time, though, the tester wants to be sure that the child offers his full thoughts and best reasons. Piaget was well aware of this problem, but he gave no indication of controlling for it experimentally. Also, in the books which first were translated into English, it appeared that Piaget based his conclusions on small samples of children and rarely subjected his results to statistical analysis. One would have thought that a red flag had been waved in the face of a scientific bull. American psychologists challenged the theory, but discovered that while Piaget's methods may have been different, he was clearly an astute observer of children. His *descriptions* of the various responses children exhibit on his tasks of object permanence, classification, and conservation have all been confirmed. There is still doubt, however, about his *explanations* of the operations underlying cognitive development and about the irreversibility and order of the sequences of development, that is, about the stage theory he proposed.

The second wave of research, as represented by the studies of Bower, Kingsley and Hall, and Gelman, questioned Piaget's choice of what responses to measure and what explanations to offer for various concepts. For example, Piaget suggested that the young infant (under 4 months) does not recognize that objects continue to exist even when they are not directly perceived. Bower's research on object permanence suggested the alternative interpretation that a very limited memory span prevented the infant from remembering the object. If, however, the object were hidden for a very short time, even infants only 20 days old could show some object permanence. In a similar way, Gelman's experiment presents an alternative explanation to Piaget's for the lack of conservation in some children. Piaget proposed that children did not conserve because they lacked certain mental operations, particularly reciprocation and negation. Gelman's training study suggested that some nonconservers had the necessary mental skills to conserve once they had learned which quantitative dimension was relevant.

Both Bower's and Gelman's studies demonstrated that if Piaget's tasks were changed in particular ways, children would exhibit certain levels of cognitive development at younger ages than had been previously suggested. Let us now examine briefly the role of ages in Piaget's system and then turn to a consideration of stage theory in general and Piaget's stage theory in particular.

It has probably been fairly obvious that few references have been made concerning the ages when children attain the various levels in Piaget's system. Piaget's writings do mention typical ages when he observed the various conservation and classification tasks to be solved. Only those who misinterpret Piaget's position to be strictly maturational would insist that hard-and-fast age ranges should be established. Piaget himself did not take that position. He was interested in describing the sequences and processes of cognitive development, not in establishing norms of development or in rank-ordering children as the intelligence testing movement has done. It was the characteristic errors children made that guided Piaget's research. Age, then, becomes of secondary importance, serving only as a general guideline to the probable level of development of a child.

STAGE THEORY

Of primary importance is the concept of *stages* of development. As noted at the beginning of this chapter, some responses are thought to be important enough and different enough from preceding responses to warrant being considered the defining characteristics of a stage or period of development. Recall the time when the infant attempts to repeat interesting events involving external objects. This was considered to be sufficiently different from the previous response pattern, repeating interesting events involving only the infant's own body, that a new stage of development was indicated. Similarly the acquisition of conservation of number was considered to be one of the defining characteristics separating the Preoperational Period from the Concrete Operational Period.

So far it must appear that stage theory is merely a convenient descriptive summary of a child's level of development. If we test a child and find him capable of certain behaviors but not others, we can then say that he is in one stage of development rather than another. This is probably more accurate than judging a child solely on the basis of his chronological age, but it is of limited value because it is merely descriptive.

Stage theory gains explanatory power (and simultaneously becomes controversial) when it is expanded to include several additional features. One such feature is the requirement that stages follow one another in a particular invariant order because the cognitive skills underlying one stage of development are prerequisites for the next stage. Invariance of order in many cases seems intuitively logical. For example, the child must be able to classify objects (e.g., in the multiple classification task) before he can compare various classifications (e.g., in the class inclusion task).

In other cases the invariance of a particular developmental sequence described by Piaget arises from empirical evidence without any logical basis. For example, conservation of *mass* has been found to develop before conservation of *weight* (Elkind, 1961). If stage theory can explain what processes control these sequences of stages, then it will become a more powerful research tool.

A second feature of some stage theories is that the sequence of stages is irreversible. This can be interpreted to mean that once a child is capable of a more mature form of a behavior, he should not normally revert to less mature responses. For example, after a child has acquired conservation of number, he should not exhibit a time when he regularly fails to show conservation of number. Yet this appears to happen. Mehler and Bever (1967) have shown that children aged 2 years–6 months to 3 years–2 months and 4 years–0 months to 4 years–7 months are more likely to conserve number than children aged 3 years–8 months to 3 years–11 months. The stipulation requiring absolute irreversibility would thus seem untenable. For Piaget, a stage represented the highest level of attainment possible, without the requirement that the child perform at this highest level at all times. It would seem necessary now for researchers to examine the conditions that regulate the child's level of performance within a stage.

There are several other controversial issues (such as the proportion of time spent *in* a stage versus time spent in transition *between* stages) that will not be discussed here. The interested reader can refer to Flavell (1971) for a good analysis of these issues in stage theory.

Piaget's writings are voluminous and the research he has stimulated is equally vast and far-reaching. The scope is too broad, however, for us to consider more of it here. Instead, let us summarize the main points of Piaget's theory and then turn our attention to a description of cognitive development in terms of processes of thinking.

SUMMARY

Piaget proposed the theoretical constructs of adaptation (assimilation and accommodation) and organization to account for the basic ways in which a person uses his schemes (behavioral patterns) to interact with his environment. These processes were viewed as invariant over age. That is, at every age a person organizes and adapts to his environment. Although the particular balance between these forces depends upon biological maturation, prior experience, and the way in which the task is presented, the processes themselves are viewed as unchanging. What does change with age are the behavioral schemes (e.g., coordination of secondary reactions) and the mental operations (e.g., identity or reciprocation) available for use in any particular problem. The acquisition of certain schemes and operations defines the various stages and periods through which all children are believed to pass. For simplification, one could say that acquiring symbolic functions marks the change from the Sensorimotor Period to the Preoperational Period; acquiring the operations which permit conservation of number and classification signals the shift into the Concrete Operational Period; and the abstract reasoning abilities which permit contrary-to-fact hypothesis generation and systematic hypothesis testing indicate the Formal Operational Period.

3

A PROCESS APPROACH
TO COGNITIVE DEVELOPMENT

The preceding chapter traced Piaget's conceptualization of cognitive development. This chapter presents a different system for organizing and describing the course of cognitive development, a system arising from the American experimental research tradition in child psychology. Unlike Piaget's theory, which was derived from one man's astute observations of his own children, the approach dealt with in this chapter draws on experimental evidence accumulated by many investigators, working on a variety of topics, and sometimes using rats, pigeons, and even adults rather than children as experimental subjects. Research is, therefore, a more integral aspect of this approach. Since no one person has developed a theory that encompasses the entire experimental literature, we shall refer to this body of information as the *process approach* to cognitive development. The discussion is not about a single process, however, but actually covers four processes, each of which contributes to the activity we call thinking. The organization for this chapter follows one suggested by Kagan (1971 b) and also found in Mussen, Conger, and Kagan (1974).

Four basic processes combine to form the activity we

call thinking. These four processes (perception, memory, generation and testing of hypotheses, and evaluation) occur at all ages, but they develop to a greater extent as children get older. For example, the number of items which a child can remember and his techniques for trying to put items explicitly into storage might change with age, but at any age, memory is a process for storing and retrieving information. Similarly, the other three processes of thought are common to people of all ages but their specific level of functioning changes, so that problem-solving or thinking appears to differ with age.

The four processes have to process something. Memory has to store some event; perception has to perceive some item. These items or events are the elements of thought, the cognitive units, on which the processes of thought operate. We will describe four cognitive units (schemata, symbols, concepts, and rules) before we consider the four processes which use the units.

UNITS OF THOUGHT

I. SCHEMATA

The first unit of thought, called *schema* (plural: schemata),* is a mental representation of events in the world. While it is intuitively obvious that adults and older children have mental representations, we need to ask whether very young infants can represent events mentally. As noted previously, an infant's behavioral repertoire is quite limited. In response to a simple question, the older, verbal child (and many adults) will produce a voluminous catalog of his knowledge. The preverbal infant rarely responds to the question, so we must infer what an infant knows by measuring phenomena we believe to be related to his knowledge. Jeffrey (1968) and McCall (1971) have suggested that a phenomenon called *habituation* could be used as an indication that an infant has schemata.

In experiments using habituation, the infant is presented with a stimulus, say a black circle on a white background.

---

* Note that this term is different from *scheme* (plural: *schemes*), which is Piaget's term for an organized pattern of behavior. The similarity of these words is unfortunate but cannot be avoided.

The infant attends visually to this stimulus (i.e., he looks at it). There are some physiological indications that he is attending, such as changes in heart rate and breathing rate, as well as his visual fixations. Each time we repeat the presentation, however, the infant spends less and less time looking at the circle. Changes in his breathing and heart rate also decrease as the stimulus is repetitively presented. The stimulus has become familiar to the infant and, in technical terminology, we would say that he has habituated to it. In nontechnical terms we would say that he is bored. The decline in interest is not just due to general fatigue, because presenting a new stimulus, say a red square on a blue background, will evoke the same magnitude of responding that the infant showed to the original stimulus. This renewed attention is called *dishabituation*. We infer that the infant has some idea of the black circle on white, some way of mentally representing that event, otherwise he could not remember from one presentation to the next what he had just seen. He would not show habituation to the black circle and dishabituation to the red square unless he could represent at least the most distinctive or important elements of the events. The term *schema* refers to this elementary memory. The habituation experiment has been used to test systematically for which features of a stimulus are critical to an individual's schemata. The general procedure is to allow the individual to habituate to a stimulus. Then one feature would be changed (e.g., its size or color or shape) and the experimenter would see if that change resulted in dishabituation. If it did, then he would conclude that this feature was part of the person's schemata.

In one experiment, Cohen, Gelber, and Lazar (1971) presented four-month-old infants with pictures of red circles for 16 trials. Then they presented two trials each with a new color but the old shape (green circles), a new shape but the old color (red triangles), and a new color with a new shape (green triangles). Dishabituation was greatest when both shape and color were changed, but dishabituation was also produced by the new color alone and the new shape alone. From a later experiment, Cohen (1973) concluded that infants stored individual stimulus components (colors and shapes) rather than specific color-shape combinations because infants who had habituated to red circles and green triangles did not dishabituate to red triangles and green circles.

Schemata, then, are stored conceptualizations of experiences, ways of organizing or classifying prior sensory events. They are not necessarily pictorial representations (as are images), nor are they tied to language. They are probably made up of the most important or distinctive elements from an experience, perhaps like a caricature or blueprint of the distinguishing features. Because schemata are closely related to direct sensory impressions, they are used primarily by infants and very young children. The other three units of thought (symbols, concepts, and rules) are more abstract mental representations, accessible to older children and adults. We shall now consider each of them in turn.

II. SYMBOLS

Symbols are arbitrary expressions or representations which stand for other things. Language is our most pervasive symbol system, and most of the sounds we produce bear only an arbitrary relation to their referents. For example, *book* is no more like the object you are currently reading than is *livre,* the French word for book. Although a few words, like *buzz, chickadee,* and *bow-wow,* are onomonopeic, most words are not.

Nonlinguistic symbols include the red cross to stand for hospital aid; yellow lines to divide highway traffic flowing in opposite directions; and a red bar over a picture of a cigarette to indicate that smoking is prohibited. You might recall that symbolic functions were discussed in some detail under Piaget's Preoperational Period. The theme of that discussion was that the presence of symbolic functions can be inferred from delayed imitation, language, symbolic play, and the search for hidden objects.

III. CONCEPTS

Symbols generally represent one specific event. *Concepts,* on the other hand, represent the attributes common to several different events. Concepts thus stand for the common elements among a group of schemata or symbols. If the word *car* means the first automobile you owned, then *car* is being used as a symbol. If, however, *car* stands for all four-wheeled vehicles of a given size, then *car* is used as a concept. Proper names are nearly always symbols (Samantha Snorkelfinger is one of a kind), but they can be concepts (John Q. Public). We often modify a concept (e.g., a delightful child) to transform it into a symbol (that delightful child who threw a rock through your window). Because children use symbols and concepts in their speech, adults are often lulled into thinking that children are speaking "their language." That children are not is apparent when we examine four developmental changes in the use of concepts. These changes involve a concept's validity, status, accessibility, and relativity.

Validity is a measure of how well the child's use of a concept agrees with the usage by the larger social community. It has been suggested that children who do not give a conservation of number response to Piaget's tasks have concepts of number and equality different from those of the adult community. The adult's concepts are based on numerosity; the child's concepts may be based on perceived length or shape. As a child develops, his understanding of a concept approaches the adult meaning; the concept becomes more valid.

The second way that concept usage shows developmental change involves how precisely and exactly the concept is used, its *status*. A three-year-old's concept of time is likely to be vague and imprecise. When his mother tells

Figure 3-1a. Typical cards used in Twenty Questions

eagle	spoon	orange	dog
apple	zebra	shovel	pitcher
teapot	ball	duck	banana
kite	sprinkling can	monkey	balloon
rake	owl	wagon	bucket
cat	pear	knife	sparrow

Figure 3-1 b. Twenty Questions pictures in a random array

him that they will go to the zoo "in two hours," he might go off and play for ten minutes and then ask if it is time to go. He has a valid concept of time since he knows that "in two hours" is sometime in the future, but he does not know exactly how much time is indicated. A ten-year-old may be no less impatient to go, but he knows more precisely when "two hours" has elapsed.

The third change in usage involves the *accessibility* of a concept, that is, how easily the child can use a concept in his thinking and how well he can communicate with others about the concept. Consider a variation on the children's game of Twenty Questions. The child is shown a set of pictures (see Figure 3-1) and told to find out which one the experimenter has in mind by asking questions that can be answered by "yes" or "no." Young children about six years old typically just guess specific items: "Is it the zebra?" or "Is it the balloon?" When the pictures are rearranged, as in Figure 3-2, the children are more likely to ask questions involving concepts: "Is it yellow?" or "Is it a toy?" (Ault,

brown eagle	brown sparrow	brown dog	brown monkey
black owl	black duck	black cat	black zebra
round apple	round orange	round ball	round balloon
yellow pear	yellow banana	yellow kite	yellow wagon
straight-handled spoon	straight-handled knife	straight-handled rake	straight-handled shovel
round-handled teapot	round-handled pitcher	round-handled bucket	round-handled sprinkling can

Figure 3-2. Twenty Questions pictures in an ordered array

1973; Van Horn & Bartz, 1968). Obviously six-year-olds have the concepts of yellow and toy, but these concepts are not as readily available as they are for older children. Increasing a concept's accessibility means increasing the chances that a child will use the concept as he solves problems. An increased accessibility of concepts is also apparent in the greater verbal skills of the older child who can talk about one concept by using other concepts. For example, an older child is more likely to discuss the concept of justice by referring to the concepts of fairness and truth. A younger child might discuss justice by referring to specific instances, such as the spanking his sister got for hitting him.

Finally as the child develops, he learns to employ concepts that are *relative* rather than absolute. If one person is taller than another, he can simultaneously be shorter than a third person. To a young child who thinks in absolute terms, the expression "dark yellow" is contradictory because yellow is a light color. He does not understand that there are many shades of yellow, some of which are darker than others.

We have just outlined four developmental changes involving a concept's validity, status, accessibility, and relativity. In addition to these four aspects, concepts can be classified in terms of the formal dimensions: categorical-superordinate, functional-relational, functional-locational, and analytic. The easiest way to explain the meaning of these formal dimensions is to consider a task which assesses them. Kagan devised a test called the Conceptual Sorting Test for this purpose (Kagan, Rosman, Day, Albert, & Phillips, 1964). The child is shown sets of pictures, each containing three items. He is asked to pick the two which "are alike in some way" and explain the basis for his choice. One set of pictures from the test includes a man, a watch, and a ruler. A categorical-superordinate grouping would be formed by the watch and the ruler, because both are measuring devices. A functional-relational response would group the man and the watch, because the man wears the watch. If the child groups the watch and the ruler because both are found in the house, a functional-locational response is indicated. An analytic response is based on some similarity of detail, such as the watch and the ruler both have numbers. Thus the reason given by the child for his particular grouping is important in determining which dimension of a concept he has used.

After testing many children, Kagan concluded that preschool children preferred to make functional-relational groupings whereas older children formed categorical-superordinate and analytic groupings (Kagan et al., 1964). Therefore he proposed that functional-relational and functional-locational groupings were less mature responses than categorical-superordinate and analytic groupings. Recent research efforts, however, have contradicted this idea.

Glick (1969) presented Kpelle (West African) rice farmers with an array of familiar objects and asked them to sort the objects into groups that belonged together. The farmers tended to sort on the basis of the functional-relational dimension. For example, a gazelle and a leaf were placed together because the gazelle eats the leaf. The farmers did not form many categorical-superordinate groups, such as a gazelle and a zebra because both are animals. While some investigators would have drawn the conclusion that Kpelle adults were at a low level of cognitive development (equal to American children), Glick was not convinced that the Kpelle adults were less developed than American adults. So, he asked them why they had sorted as they did. They replied that "this was the clever way to do it, the way that made 'Kpelle sense.' " Glick then asked them to sort the items the way a stupid Kpelle might, and they made perfect categorical-superordinate categories comparable to those made by American adults. Obviously, each culture has its own definition of cleverness and teaches its people to respond in the clever manner. Furthermore, tests with American children have systematically varied aspects of the testing situation, such as whether the stimuli are pictures or words, and obtained correspondingly different proportions of categorical, analytic, and functional responses (Olver & Hornsby, 1966). The important point is that children must learn to use these formal dimensions of concepts.

The differences between children's use of concepts and adults' can be seen in situations involving word associations. The free-association technique ("Say the first word you think of in response to my word") has been used in psychoanalysis, as a parlor game, and as a method of assessing children's language development. Researchers studying language development have identified a progression in the types of responses children will give in the free-association situation. In the early preschool years, children

will try to find a rhyme to the stimulus word, without regard for the meaningfulness of their response. For example,
in response to *sun,* the preschooler might say *run* or *lun.*
A few years later, the child's typical response is to answer
with a word that logically follows or precedes the stimulus
word in a sentence, such as *sun-shine* or *sun-hot.* Still later,
the adult pattern emerges. That pattern is to respond with
the same part of speech, frequently with a synonym or
antonym. To *sun,* most older children and adults respond
*moon.**

* I remember my mother's reluctant acceptance of my offers to help
her solve newspaper crossword puzzles. She was well aware of my
childish word associations.

IV. RULES

We now come to the fourth unit of thought, *rules*. Rules are statements which specify a relationship between two or more concepts. Some rules are informal, expressing a relation which is generally true (e.g., "Mommy is nice") but which can be violated (e.g., "Mommy just spanked me"). Other rules are formal and always true, such as the rule of arithmetic, 2 + 2 = 4. An example of a rule which we have already examined in some detail is conservation. "Number does not change when shape is manipulated" is a formal rule which the conserving child has acquired but the nonconserving child has not. Even when a child realizes that the rules he uses are not completely accurate, he will be reluctant to abandon them until he has some new rule to replace the old one.

Consider an example of rule-learning in language acquisition. When children learn that past tense verbs are formed by adding *ed* to the present tense verb (e.g., I walk; I walked), they generalize this rule to all situations (e.g., I run; I runned). Eventually they learn that many past tense verbs are irregular (e.g., I run; I ran). If they do not know the proper form for a particular verb, even though they know it is irregular, they may produce an incorrect, but rule-governed form. Recall the eight-year-old described in the previous chapter who said, "All you did was spreaded them out."

In addition to categorizing rules as formal or informal, rules can be classified as transformational or nontransformational on the basis of whether the rule specifies what happens when two concepts are combined (transformational) or merely whether several concepts are related (nontransformational). The following statements are examples of transformational rules: "Mix flour, water, and eggs to make a cake" and "Multiply the length by the width to obtain an area." These rules require the person to "operate" or act on the elements to obtain the product. Nontransformational rules, like "Fire is hot" and "A square has four equal sides," do not prescribe any action. Younger children do not spontaneously apply transformational rules; they are likely to exhibit relatively unsystematic trial-and-error learning. Since transformational rules considerably simplify problem-solving, as children develop, they employ transformational rules in preference to nontransformational rules or no rules. It is probably no coincidence that algebra and chemistry problems, which depend upon transformational rules more than other academic topics, are not taught until junior or senior high school.

In summary, cognitive processes operate with four units of thought: schemata, symbols, concepts, and rules. Several major shifts occur in the child's use of these units. One such developmental change is from using primarily schemata to using symbols, concepts (especially language), and rules. In another change, concepts gain increased validity, status, and accessibility, and the child learns to use concepts relatively as well as absolutely. Another shift with age involves the particular rule a child tries to use in solving problems. The more precisely the rule applies to a particular situation, the more likely the child will arrive at the correct solution. These developmental changes in the units of thought are closely related to the development of the processes of thought, which we shall examine next.

PROCESSES OF THOUGHT

It is virtually impossible to discuss thinking as a whole complex phenomena, like thinking, as a single unit; but it can be misleading to separate the phenomenon into its components, especially when the pieces are interrelated or overlap. Four processes of thought are presented in this chapter, but you should remember that distinctions between them frequently blur. Historically, three of the processes (perception, memory, and hypothesis testing) have been topics of extensive research. The fourth (evaluation) is less well studied.

I. PERCEPTION

Perception can be defined as "the process by which the child extracts meaningful information from the meaningless mosaic of physical stimulation" (Mussen, Conger, and Kagan, 1974, p. 278). Physical stimulation in the visual system, for example, is a pattern of lightwaves of varying wavelengths, intensities, and directions of source. Processing by the eye, optic nerve, and visual cortex in the brain produces direct information about the physical stimulus. Perception combines this direct information, additional information obtained from memory concerning similar previous sensations, and information about what the person expected to see. The result is a meaningful product called the perception of the situation. Perception is thus both a process and the final product of that process.

In addition to perceiving individual physical properties of objects, such as color, texture, and shape, a person can also perceive whole patterns of properties and thereby distinguish the identity of a particular example from a class of similar objects. For example, the avid birdwatcher can identify that pattern which is the yellow-bellied sapsucker even in a tree full of other birds. Individuals also perceive spatial relations between objects (e.g., one thing is to the left of another), events which arise from stimulation over time (e.g., a closing door is seen as one continuous object, not a series of discrete doors), two-dimensional representations (e.g., pictures of three-dimensional objects), and symbolic codes. The two most prominent symbolic codes that a child must learn to perceive are the phonemes which make up spoken language and the graphemes of written language. For example, the child has to perceive the difference in sound between "Tad" and "Dad" when he has to decide whether to throw the ball to his brother or father. Similarly, the child must perceive the difference between *b* and *d* to read *bed* and *deb* correctly.

Perception is important in problem-solving because the solutions that a child attempts will depend upon the information that he has available, which, in turn, is a function of (a) his attention to particular aspects of the problem and (b) his prior experiences. Because these two factors influence the perceptual process, we will now examine both of them in greater detail.

Attention

The amount of physical stimulation available to a person is truly overwhelming. Sights, sounds, odors, touch cues, etc. continually bombard our sensory organs. Yet, we seem to take notice of only a fraction of them because we have the ability to attend selectively. At a very noisy party, we can listen to the one conversation directed at us while we ignore all the other conversations. This example of selective attention is called the cocktail party phenomenon. Selective attention is also demonstrated when children are so engrossed in a game that they do not hear their mother calling them.*

Although children of all ages exhibit some selective attention, the capability becomes refined with increased age, permitting the older child to eliminate highly attractive distractions better than a younger child. An experimental task which shows the superior selective attention of older children was developed by Stroop (1935). In one variation of this task, children are asked to read aloud the printed names of various colors. Sometimes the names are printed in black and sometimes they are printed in various colors.

* Parents frequently prefer the explanation that children show selective oblivion.

Thus, the word *red* might be printed in yellow letters. The child is either asked to name the color of the letters or to read the word. If he is asked to name the color of the letters, the word that the letters spell is a distracting cue and the cause of more naming errors in younger children than in older children. Santostafano and Paley (1964) have demonstrated the same phenomenon using normally or incongruously colored pictures of fruits.

The length of time that a child will remain at a task (his attention span) also increases with age. For this reason teachers often program only 10 minutes of an academic activity with nursery school children, 30 minutes with grade school children, and 60 minutes with high school students. As you know from your own experiences, some activities are more attractive than others, so the length of time you attend to them varies accordingly. Most children will play outside much longer than they will practice on the piano. An infant will play with a rattle much longer than will a college professor (at least, most college professors), but if one takes into consideration the appeal of the activity for the individual, then the older child's attention span, on the whole, is longer.

Another developmental change in attention involves the speed with which a child can redirect his attention. Because older children can redirect their attention faster than younger children can, the older child is better able to shift his focus between the different aspects of a task. A very rapid shift in focus may result in the perception of a relationship between the different aspects that would not otherwise be apparent. Perhaps this is equivalent to saying that a person can hold two facets of a task in mind simultaneously. Piaget explained successful performance on the class inclusion problem by stating that the child attended to both the parts and the whole at the same time. An alternative explanation is that the successful child shifts his attention between the parts and the whole so rapidly that he perceives the relationship between them.

Prior Experience

Perception is faster and more accurate in older children because they have a broader range of experiences on which to base their expectations. Even information that is incomplete triggers associations that set the person to expect one thing instead of another. The more prior associations a person has, the more likely that he has a perceptual set which will match incomplete incoming information.* Older children are therefore more likely to predict an event from partial information. For example, they have a higher success rate in identifying a picture when only parts of the drawing are made visible (Gollin, 1960; 1962). (See Figure 3-3 for an illustration of partial drawings.)

In addition to building up expectations, prior experience facilitates perceptual learning. Until recently, two theories of perceptual learning were seen as competing. One theory (variously called the *schema hypothesis* or the *enrichment theory*) proposed that each time a person perceived an object, a small amount of information was added to the previous schema of that object (e.g., Bruner, 1957; Vernon, 1955). Practice or prior experience thus enables the subject to build up a better schema of each stimulus. The sensations that arise directly from the stimulus are meaningless until these sensations are enriched by information from other sources, such as schemata. If the subject's task is to discriminate between two stimuli, then he must compare the schemata associated with each stimulus. If the sche-

* Perceptual sets do not always improve perceptual performance. Occasionally a perceptual set will suggest an incorrect perception that is strong enough to block the correct perception even when further information confirms that the first perception was incorrect.

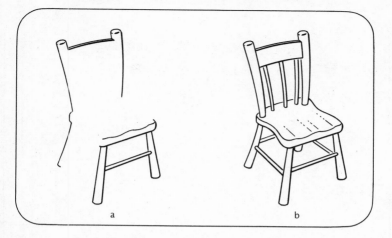

Figure 3-3. Partially completed drawings of a chair.

a. The older child is likely to recognize the stimulus as a chair;
b. the younger child must see more of the stimulus to recognize it.

mata of the two stimuli match, then the subject cannot distinguish between them. If the schemata are different, then he can discriminate between them. The greater the amount of information associated with the schemata, the more likely a comparison of the schemata will yield the correct decision. Let us consider an example in which a child is presented with four stimuli: the letters *b, d, p,* and *q.* If the child has had little exposure to letters, he might form identical schemata for all four letters, as shown in Figure 3-4a. With more experience, the child might form the second set of schemata shown in Figure 3-4b. This set has added the information that the loops are at the top or bottom of the straight line. This set would not allow the child to distinguish *b* from *d* or *p* from *q,* but it would allow him to distinguish *b* or *d* from *p* or *q.* Finally, the child might

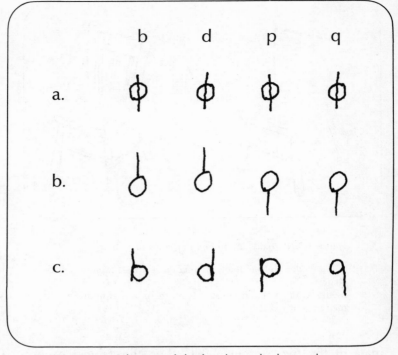

Figure 3-4. Schemata of the four letters b, d, p, and q.

construct the schemata in Figure 3-4c, adding the information about the left-right orientation of the loop relative to the line. Now all four letters can be distinguished. One point about this example needs to be clarified. The drawings in Figure 3-4a have been oversimplified and give the incorrect impression that they are exact images of the stimuli, but that is not the intention. Schemata are not simple graphic images.

The alternative theory (called *differentiation theory* or the *distinctive features hypothesis*) proposed that stimuli give rise to very complex and meaningful perceptions rather than to meager sensations. The process of perception is abstracting small amounts of information from this very rich source.

Each time a person perceives an object, he detects features or relationships that he did not notice before. Practice or prior experience teaches the person which features or patterns of features are distinctive and critical for identification. Perceptions thus become more differentiated, increasing the degree of correspondence between the potential stimulus information and the perception of that information (Gibson, 1969). Let us return to the examples of the four letters. The child with little prior exposure to the letters might decide that the distinctive features of the stimuli were the presence of a line and a loop, as diagrammed in Figure 3-5a. Since these two characteristics are irrelevant to this discrimination, the four letters would not be distinguished. With more experience, the loop's position at the top or bottom of the line might be selected as an important feature (see Figure 3-5b). Finally, the feature of left-right orientation is noted (see Figure 3-5c) and all four letters are distinguished. We should note that efficient perception also requires that irrelevant information be ignored. In terms of our previous example—with experience, unnecessary details such as the size or color of the letter can be deleted.

The differentiation theory and the enrichment theory are now seen as complimentary rather than conflicting (Stevenson, 1972). That is, subjects can build up a mental representation of a stimulus event (a schema) and they can pick out the distinctive features of a stimulus. It seems likely that when a subject must make an identification of one stimulus, he compares it with various schemata and picks the best match. When the subject is asked to distinguish among several stimuli simultaneously, he can isolate their distinctive features. Recall that schemata are not a.　　b → straight line and loop

　　　　d → straight line and loop

　　　　p → straight line and loop

　　　　q → straight line and loop

b.　　b → loop at bottom of line

　　　　d → loop at bottom of line

　　　　p → loop at top of line

　　　　q → loop at top of line

c.　　b → loop at bottom-right of line

　　　　d → loop at bottom-left of line

　　　　p → loop at top-right of line

　　　　q → loop at top-left of line

Figure 3-5. Feature sets associated with the letters *b, d, p,* and *q.*

just exact images of the stimulus. It may be that "schemata are composed of distinctive features . . . when many distinctive features have been stored, one has a 'refined' schemata" (Caldwell & Hall, 1970, p. 7).

The perceptual process does not function in isolation of the other processes of thought. Perceptions are stored in memory and information is recalled from memory to help interpret incoming perceptions. Hence we need to examine memory as the second process of thought.

II. MEMORY

When we store some aspect of an experience for a period of time after the experience has occurred, we have engaged the process of memory. There are two conceptual frameworks for discussing memory. The first, more traditional one, is concerned with three storage systems: sensory memory, short-term memory, and long-term memory. The second, more recent one, focuses on levels (or depths) of processing. Although most of the research on children's memory has come from the traditional orientation, the levels of processing approach is likely to gain in popularity as it becomes more familiar to researchers.

1. Storage Systems

Sensory Memory
Sensory memory is the briefest of the three storage systems, lasting only about $1/4$ of a second. A test for this aspect of memory was devised by Sperling (1960). He used a device called a tachistoscope to show subjects a visual stimulus consisting of nine letters, arranged in three rows of three each, for a very brief period of time (50 msec.).

Typically subjects would report four or five of the letters. Two explanations for this level of performance seemed probable. Either the subject had seen only four or five letters and reported everything in his memory, or the subject had seen all nine letters but forgotten some of them before he could report them all. The latter hypothesis was supported when Sperling changed the procedure slightly. He prearranged a signal system with the subjects so that a high tone indicated they should report the top row of letters, a middle tone indicated they should report the middle row, and a low tone indicated the bottom row. Then, *after* the visual stimulus was turned off, one tone was played. Subjects were able to report the one appropriate row quite easily. Thus they must have seen all nine letters. When the tone sounded, they scanned their sensory memory and reported the letters in that row. The image must fade very quickly though, because even a delay of $1/4$ second in sounding the tone resulted in much poorer performance.

Since we know that many memories last longer than $1/4$ second, a distinction can be made between sensory memory and the longer storage systems. Researchers currently believe that both children and adults have the same sensory memory system, so any developmentally related differences in memory performance are attributed to differences in short-term or long-term memory systems.

Short-term Memory
Short-term memory is longer than sensory memory, lasting up to 30 seconds, but it is still transitory in the sense that information can be lost during that time. We use short-term memory when we need to remember a phone number just long enough to dial it, or to remember the purchase price of an item just long enough to get out our money. If adults try to remember a random sequence of items such as digits or nonsense syllables immediately after

hearing the items, they can usually recall about seven items (Miller, 1956).* Five-year-olds can recall at most about five items, and younger children recall even fewer. Thus, changes in the capacity of short-term memory occur with increasing age.

If we need to keep information in short-term memory longer than 30 seconds, we can rehearse the material. In other words, we can repeat it over and over, continually re-entering it into short-term memory. Children less than about seven years old do not spontaneously use rehearsal, which is a contributing factor to why the memory of younger children appears to be less than that of older children (Flavell, Beach, & Chinsky, 1966). When young children are instructed to rehearse, they can do so, and their recall scores improve correspondingly.

In a study of short-term memory and rehearsal, Kingsley and Hagen (1969) taught some nursery school children labels for nonsense figures drawn on cards like those in Figure 3-6. Then the children played a card game like "Concentration." One at a time, five cards were shown to a child and then turned face down in a row. (See Figure 3-7.) Next a cue card, identical to one of the stimulus cards, was presented. The child's task was to select the matching card from the face-down row. The experimental group relevant to this discussion was required to label each stimulus card as it was presented and to rehearse these labels, starting from the beginning of the row, after each new card was presented. In remembering the location of the matching card, children in this group performed significantly better than children in two other groups who labeled the cards as they were presented but did not rehearse or who neither labeled nor rehearsed the cards.

---

* The capacity of short-term memory can be increased if one organizes the material into "chunks," a technique which will be discussed more fully under long-term memory.

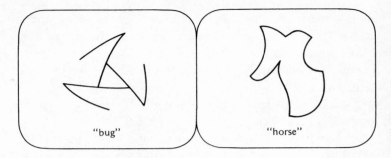

Figure 3-6. Two nonsense figures and their labels, from an experiment by Kingsley and Hagen (1969).

The superiority of the subjects who rehearsed was most apparent when the matching card had been presented first (and therefore had to be kept in memory for the longest time). The authors concluded that nursery school children do not spontaneously name or repeat items to be remembered in a memory task, but if they are helped to do so, their memory scores improve.

In fact, rehearsal is not even a preferred mnemonic strategy until children are about in fifth grade. Kreutzer, Leonard, and Flavell (1975) interviewed children from the kindergarten, first, third, and fifth grades, asking questions about what the children knew about their own memory processes. For example, the children were asked:

(1) If you wanted to phone your friend and someone told you the phone number, would it make any difference if you called right away after you heard the number or if you got a drink of water first? (2) Why? (3) What do you do when you want to remember a phone number? [p. 9]

Even some of the kindergarten children knew that some things could be forgotten rapidly. By first grade, over half the children said they should phone first or else they might forget the number. In response to the third part of the

Figure 3-7. Procedure in Kingsley and Hagen's experiment.

a. Experimenter presents third card to subject.

b. Experimenter presents cue card. Subject must turn over middle card to be correct.

question, the most common strategy offered for aiding memory relied on external prompts, either writing down the number or having someone else (i.e., Mother) remind them of it. The following answer from a third grader reflects an attempt to devise a self-generated prompt.

> Say the number is 633-8854. Then what I'd do is—say that my number is 633, so I won't have to remember that, really. And then I would think, now I've got to remember 88. Now I'm 8 years old, so I can remember, say, my age two times. And then I say how old my brother is, and how old he was last year. And that's how I'd usually remember that phone number. (Is that how you would most often remember a phone number?) Well, usually I write it down. [p. 11]

Only at fifth grade did some of the children think of verbal rehearsal as a deliberate memory strategy. They knew that they should repeat the number several times, and that the last four numbers would be harder to remember than the first three, which might be the same exchange as their own number.

Long-term Memory
Long-term memory is different from sensory and short-term memory in several important ways. First, it is not limited to fewer than ten unrelated items as the other two memory systems are. All the memories we have of our childhood, of last year, of last week, etc. are stored in long-term memory. Second, items in long-term memory do not decay automatically in a short period of time. Whether items can ever be permanently lost from long-term memory or are just temporarily inaccessible is a long-standing, unresolved topic of research. In either case, items do not decay rapidly. Third, special effort is required to put items into long-term memory. Traditional theories of memory postulated that events entered long-term memory after being processed by short-term memory. Some current

theorists hypothesize that the two memory systems are at least partially independent and function in a parallel fashion (Kesner, 1973; Posner, 1973).

We have already mentioned one technique, rehearsal, which is a special effort for putting items into long-term memory. Sheer repetition seems to increase the probability that an item will enter long-term memory. Another technique, called imagery, is to imagine a distinctive picture which either includes the item which is to be remembered or symbolizes it. If you need to remember that the term "Concrete Operations" refers to Piaget's third period of development, you might imagine *three* surgeons *operating* on a slab of *concrete*. (See Figure 3-8.) Imagery can be used more easily for some memory tasks than others because some terms evoke images more readily than others. For example, most Americans probably form a similar image of the Washington Monument (see Figure 3-9) but their images of freedom depend on their perspective. (See Figure 3-10.) Concepts that easily evoke images are said to be more concrete than concepts which do not. There are also individual differences in people's ability to form images. A clinical procedure called systematic desensitization relies on the client's ability to imagine feared objects or feared situations to help eliminate or reduce those fears. Some people have such poor visualization skills that they cannot participate in this form of therapy.

A third technique for putting items into long-term memory is called chunking (Miller, 1956). Chunking involves finding some higher-order category to which several of the items belong and organizing our storage and retrieval of information according to these categories. Let us say, for example, that a child needed to remember the following list: zebra, cow, dog, pig, horse, balloon, kite, wagon, ball, yo-yo, car, truck, plane, bus, and boat. If he tried to remember the list without any organizing principle, he

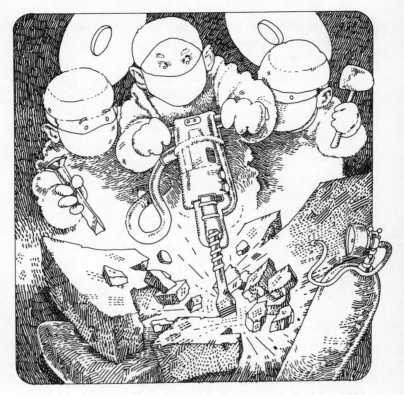

Figure 3-8. An image of three doctors operating on concrete, to symbolize Piaget's third period of development, the Concrete Operational Period.

would probably only recall 5 to 9 words, the limit imposed by short-term memory. If he recognized, however, that the list includes five animals, five toys, and five vehicles, he might succeed in remembering 12 to 15 words. Chunking the information into higher-order groups makes it easier to handle by providing an organized method for remembering.

Just as young children fail to use rehearsal spontane-

Figure 3-9. Image of the Washington Monument.

ously, they also do not use chunking. Moely, Olson, Halwes, and Flavell (1969) demonstrated that kindergarten, first- and third-grade children did not spontaneously chunk items either while they examined the stimulus items or later during recall. With instructions on chunking, however, even the kindergarten children could do so, and their memory scores improved considerably.

The memory tests referred to so far have all been *recall* tests. In a recall task, the subject has to generate the test items with no clues from the experimenter. In the easier

Figure 3-10. Images of freedom.

recognition test, the experimenter supplies a mixture of test items and novel items. The subject's task is to identify which items he has been told to remember. A familiar example is a multiple-choice exam, where the person only has to recognize the alternative which is correct. Fill-in-the-blank and essay exams, on the other hand, are recall tests.

Because younger children make little use of rehearsal and chunking, their memory on recognition tests is much greater than on recall tests. In one experiment four-year-old and ten-year-old children were shown 12 pictures to be remembered. At both ages the children could select the 12 pictures which they had seen previously out of a set of 100 pictures. On a recall test, though, the four-year-olds could recall only 2 or 3 of the pictures, whereas the ten-year-olds could recall about 8 (Kagan, Klein, Haith, & Morrison, 1973). Thus, developmental changes in memory are most noticeable on recall tests because successful performance requires the child to use deliberate techniques (rehearsal and chunking) for memorizing the material.

2. Levels of Processing

One of the novel features of the levels of processing approach to memory is that memory is a by-product of perceptual analysis. Starting from the assumption that stimuli are analyzed to varying degrees, Craik and Lockhart (1972) proposed that each of these levels of analysis gives rise to a memory trace. For example, a visual stimulus such as the word *sheep* can be perceived at a sensory level, dealing with its physical properties such as the contours of the letters, the length of the word, its type (script, italic, etc.). At deeper levels of processing, the letters are recognized as a pattern making up a word, the meaning of the word is evoked, and other associations to the word may be added.

Corresponding to these levels of perceptual analysis are levels of memory. Sensory memory traces are fleeting because the perception of physical properties does not require deep analysis. The deeper semantic analysis produces a more durable memory trace of the meaning extracted from the stimulus.

An experiment that will make these ideas clearer was conducted by Craik and Tulving (1975). They flashed words very rapidly at their subjects and asked the subjects to answer a question about the word. Some questions required only sensory analysis. For example, subjects were asked if the word was printed in capital or small letters. Other questions, such as "Does the word rhyme with leap?" evoked an intermediate level of analysis. Questions such as, "Is the word a farm animal?" required deep semantic analysis. Later the subjects were unexpectedly asked to recall or recognize all the words they had seen in the experiment. Words that had been processed at the more shallow levels were not recalled nearly as often as words that had been analyzed more deeply.

It will take some time before the levels of processing interpretation of memory is extended to include developmental data. In the meantime, this approach serves to remind the reader that new research is always necessary to advance our understanding of children. With a problem perceived and certain facts recalled from memory, the child's next task is to activate the third process of thought.

III. GENERATION AND TESTING OF HYPOTHESES

After a child recognizes that there is a problem to be solved, he can generate a set of hypotheses (possible solutions). The size of this set and the adequacy (appropriateness) of the hypotheses depend on the child's prior experience with similar problems. If the child has had many prior experiences, he can often generalize quite easily from the old problems to the new one. Thus, older children will, in general, be better able to solve a new problem merely because they have had more experience with similar problems on which to base their hypotheses. The child with a wider variety of cognitive units (schemata, images, symbols, concepts, and rules) is more likely to find a solution because he can draw on more knowledge. After a child thinks of a hypothesis (generation) he must acquire information to confirm or disconfirm it (testing).

Let us compare four hypothetical children, ages 3, 4, 5, and 6 years, to demonstrate hypothesis generation and hypothesis testing. Each child is taken to a room and is told that when he comes out of the room he can play with a toy. The experimenter then leaves the room, shutting the door behind himself. Each child immediately goes to the door, to try to open it. The three-year-old has learned one rule about doors: They can be pushed or pulled. On the basis of this one rule, he generates two hypotheses. One is that the door should be pushed; the other is that the door should be pulled. The child tests these two hypotheses, by pushing and pulling the door, but it does not open. The four-year-old has learned the same rule about pushing and pulling, but because he has had more experience with doors, he has learned a second rule: Doorknobs can be turned clockwise or counterclockwise. The four-year-old tests various hypotheses by combinations of push-

119

ing, pulling, and turning the doorknob. Eventually, he finds that he should first turn the knob clockwise and then pull the door. The five-year-old has more elaborate rules about opening doors. He knows, for example, that doorknobs almost always turn clockwise and that they must be turned before pushing or pulling. His problem is very much simpler than the three-year-old's and also easier than the four-year-old's because he has more exact rules. He only needs to generate and test the hypothesis about pushing vs. pulling. A still older child, say six years old, might have watched the experimenter leave the room and observed whether the door swung inward or outward. He could then open the door the very first time he tried, because the hypothesis he would generate to test first would be completely appropriate.

Getting out of the room depended upon the child's generating hypotheses about how doors open. When the hypotheses are insufficient, as in the case of the three-year-old, the child may never solve the problem.* If the hypotheses are more or less adequate but must be combined in novel ways, as in the cases of the four- and five-year-olds, we can observe complex hypothesis testing. When prior learning is sufficient, as in the case of the six-year-old, only one hypothesis needs to be generated and it is likely to be the correct solution. As the child accumulates experience, the expectation of correctness increases until the hypothesis is considered to be a rule. If such a hypothesis turns out to be incorrect, perhaps due to an external agent like Candid Camera or a devious experimenter, considerable consternation can result.

The example above serves as a good, practical illustration of hypothesis generation and hypothesis testing. Natural situations, however, usually contain uncontrollable as-

---

* Of course, he may generate and test one further hypothesis, that if he screams loudly enough, someone is likely to let him out.

pects, such as the exact kind of experience with doors each child has had. Researchers generally turn to artificial problems which offer greater control of unwanted variations in exchange for their lack of naturalness. We shall now turn to a few experimental studies of hypothesis generation and testing to examine the developmental changes in this process of thought. Experiments in hypothesis generation and testing can be divided into two categories. One is based on the child's verbal statements; the other analyzes a sequence of nonverbal behaviors.

A Verbal Technique—Twenty Questions

Under the topic of a concept's accessibility, we described the Twenty Questions game. The child is shown an array of pictures (refer back to Figure 3-1) and told to guess which one the experimenter has in mind by asking questions that can be answered by "yes" or "no." The questions which children ask have been classified into four types. One kind of question has been labeled a specific hypothesis. The child names one of the pictures and asks specifically about it. Examples are "Is it the kite?" and "Is it the monkey?" The specific hypothesis is obviously the least efficient question that could be asked because only one picture can be eliminated from the array with each question. A general question which can eliminate more than one alternative, on the other hand, is a constraint-seeking question. The child can fashion constraint-seeking questions along many different conceptual dimensions. Questions can refer to some perceptual feature of the objects such as their color, size, shape, or distinctive markings. Examples of such perceptual constraint-seeking questions are "Is it yellow?" or "Does it have a tail?" Other types of constraint-seeking questions may refer to an object's function ("Can you eat it?"), classification ("Is it an animal?"), location in the array ("Is it in the first row?"), etc. For the sake of simplicity, we shall call these constraint-seeking questions nonperceptual. Finally, it is useful to distinguish an intermediate type called pseudoconstraint-seeking questions. These questions appear to have the form of a constraint-seeking question but, like a specific hypothesis, refer to only one picture. Examples are "Is it like a horse but with black and white stripes?" (the zebra) and "Is it green with a flower on it?" (the sprinkling can).

The sequence for the types of questions that children of various ages will generate is well established. As you might suspect, specific hypotheses are the predominant type of questions for children under the age of six or seven years. When children learn that guessing specific pictures is "wrong," they try to use the more advanced types of questions but at first only the *form* of the question is learned. Pseudoconstraint-seeking questions, therefore, play a transitional role between specific hypotheses and constraint-seeking questions. Of the two major types of constraint-seeking questions, perceptual ones appear first, perhaps because perceptual *concepts* are more accessible to younger children. As children gain experience dealing with nonperceptual categories, they use nonperceptual constraint-seeking questions more. Whether perceptual questions are as efficient as nonperceptual questions depends on the particular set of pictures used in the game. In general, however, the nonperceptual questions will be more efficient, and this fact probably explains why children come to prefer them (Ault, 1973; Mosher & Hornsby, 1966).

We might note parenthetically that perceptual constraint-seeking questions and successful performance on Piaget's class inclusion problem appear at the same general age, about eight years old. In both tasks, the child must shift his attention back and forth between the specific elements of the set and the higher-order category to which the elements belong. In the class inclusion problem, this shift occurs between the parts (white or blue beads) and the whole (wooden beads). In the Twenty Questions game, the shift is between the specific pictures (kite, banana, pear, etc.) and the perceptual category (yellow).

The Twenty Questions game is one way of measuring change in children's hypothesis generation, but it has two drawbacks. It is dependent to some extent on a child's verbal skills, and it does not discriminate among children below the age of 6 to 7, or above the age of 11 to 12 years. In other words, its range of applicability is restricted. Because it is unreasonable to suppose that no differences exist in hypothesis generation between a three-year-old and a six-year-old, or between a twelve-year-old and a college student, researchers have used nonverbal tasks which permit a wider age range to be tested.

A Nonverbal Technique—Probability Learning

The most common probability learning task presents the subject with three buttons on a panel and some method of delivering a reward, such as a hole through which marbles can be dropped. The subject is instructed to push one button at a time. If the correct button is pushed, he gets a marble. The goal is to get as many marbles as possible in a fixed number of trials (pushes). Two of the three buttons are never correct and hence never result in marbles. The third button is partially correct. Some fraction of the time, say 33 per cent, the subject gets a marble if he pushes this button. The other 67 per cent of the time, he gets nothing after pushing this button. Obviously, a subject cannot obtain a marble on every trial. The best he can do is push the "correct" button all the time and get marbles after a third of these pushes. This strategy is called maximizing because the subject maximizes his changes of getting a marble. If he pushes either of the other two buttons, he gets fewer marbles.

Weir (1964) compiled data for 80 trials on subjects ranging in age from 3 years old to 19 years old. The 3-year-olds adopt the maximizing strategy fairly soon after the experiment begins, and by the last block of 20 trials, they push the correct button as much as 80 per cent of the time. The 19-year-olds also maximize by the last 20 trials, but they take many more trials to reach this point. At the intermediate ages, from 5 to 15 years, children push the correct button less than 50 per cent of the time, even after 80 trials. This finding is surprising since 3-year-olds rarely perform better on any task than school age children or arrive at a solution (maximizing) faster than college students. To explain these startling results, we need to examine the sequence of button-pushing which children exhibit across all the trials.

The 3-year-olds spend a few trials trying all the different buttons. Then they seem to settle on the correct button and push it most of the time. The 5- to 9-year-olds tend to adopt some alternating patterns, such as left-middle-right or right-middle-left, which yield few marbles, and the 11- to 15-year-olds sometimes formulate even more complex alternations. Why do these children persist in testing elaborate patterns when the success rate for them is so low? There are many potential reasons, but we will restrict our discussion to two major ones which emphasize (a) the expectations which children bring to the experiment and (b) the skill which the children have for generating and testing hypotheses. If children come to the task expecting a higher rate of success than is actually available, they will look for solutions which match their prior expectations. In other words, they will continue to generate patterns of responses in hope that one of these patterns will "pay off" at the expected rate, even though searching for this pattern costs them marbles. In contrast, the 3-year-olds do not expect to get marbles on every trial, perhaps because they do not generally consider themselves very successful at such tasks. They willingly settle for marbles on only 33 per cent of the trials. Older children who have expectations of finding completely correct solutions (i.e., getting marbles after every trial) continue to generate and test hypotheses, looking for a pattern of responses which they believe will earn them more marbles (Stevenson, 1972).

In addition, 3-year-olds may not generate very many hypotheses about how to push the buttons. They try each button in turn, discover that two never pay off, and so settle on the third button. Children of intermediate ages generate many elaborate hypotheses, but their ability to test these patterns is not fully developed. Their memory may not be sufficient to remember exactly which sequences have been tried or which remain to be tried. They may not organize the potential sequences in a logical way (which would help them remember where they are in their search). Moreover, they probably consider each sequence as likely as any other. Older subjects, such as the 19-year-olds, might judge that the experimenter is unlikely to choose highly idiosyncratic patterns, so such patterns need not be considered. Older children can also organize their search in a more efficient and logical manner, and they can keep better track of where they are. Thus, many college students eventually test the hypothesis that no consistent pattern for obtaining marbles exists, and they choose instead to maximize.

In the probability learning situation, the subject has virtually an unlimited number of hypotheses he can generate concerning the task's solution, and he must also devise some system for testing all of them in the number of trials allowed. The combined process of hypothesis generation and testing cannot be controlled or observed separately in probability learning tasks. If we want to see the influence of hypothesis testing alone, we must turn to a different nonverbal task, one in which the subject is given a limited set of hypotheses to choose from so that hypothesis generation is not a factor.

The Levine Blank Trials Procedure

Tasks called cue-selection problems have long been used to assess adult hypothesis testing. The basic task presents the subject with a set of dimensions (e.g., shape, color, size, etc.), each of which is represented by several values. Examine the four stimulus pairs in Figure 3-11. The four dimensions (and two values) represented are as follows: letter (*x* or *t*), size (*large* or *small*), color (*black* or *white*), and position (*left* or *right*). The subject is asked to determine which value of one of the dimensions is correct. Since the different possible values are clearly specified for the subject, hypothesis generation is not a problem; the burden falls on hypothesis testing.

Levine (1966) developed a procedure to assess which hypothesis a subject tested in the cue-selection problem. If the subject tests the same hypothesis for each of the four pairs in Figure 3-11, he will exhibit a unique pattern of left and right choices. For example, if his hypothesis is that *t* is correct, he will show a right-right-left-left pattern. If his hypothesis is that *black* is correct, he will choose right-left-right-left. In all, the subject can exhibit eight unique patterns corresponding to the eight stimulus values. Some patterns, such as right-right-right-left do not correspond to

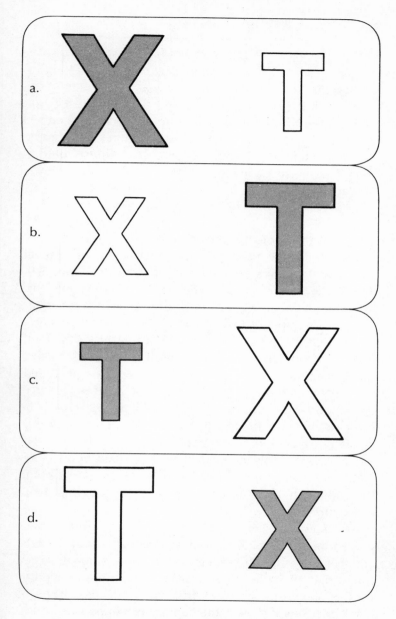

Figure 3-11. Four stimulus pairs, adapted from Figure 1, Levine (1966).

any of the eight simple hypotheses. If a subject displays one of these patterns, we cannot be sure he is testing hypotheses in any systematic way.

In another study, Levine showed that a subject would continue with one hypothesis if he received no feedback on that trial about whether he was correct or incorrect (Levine, Leitenberg, & Richter, 1964). If a subject could be given four no-feedback (or blank) trials in a row (one trial on each stimulus pair of Figure 3-11), one could infer exactly which of the eight possible hypotheses he was testing. Levine's blank trials procedure incorporated this fact by giving the subject feedback only every fifth trial. The subject is told "correct" or "incorrect" on trials 1, 6, 11, and 16 and receives no feedback following trials 2-5, 7-10, and 11-15. Moreover, once the subject receives feedback he should be able to discard half of the remaining hypotheses. For example, if the subject chose the *small, white, t, on the right* in pair a of Figure 3-11 and received the feedback "correct," he can eliminate the hypotheses *large, black, x,* and *on the left.* Let us say that on the next feedback trial (pair b of Figure 3-11) the subject chose the *large, black, t, on the right* and again was told "correct." Now he can also eliminate the hypotheses *small* and *white;* the hypotheses *t* and *on the right* remain to be tested. If the subject always discards incorrect hypotheses and never eliminates ones which are correct, he will solve the problem in the minimum number of trials. This strategy has been called "focusing."

Ingalls and Dickerson (1969) used Levine's blank trials procedure to examine hypothesis testing in fifth graders, eighth graders, tenth graders, and college students. They found that all subjects had a high rate of testing hypotheses, as shown by the blank trials data. The proportion of blank trial sets in which the subject exhibited one of the eight patterns corresponding to a consistent (but not necessarily correct) hypothesis ranged from .81 for the fifth graders to .89 for the college students.

Ingalls and Dickerson (1969) also found that focusing increased with age. When Eimas (1970) extended the study down to second graders, he found that they eliminated some hypotheses properly after the first feedback trial but did not demonstrate further focusing on later trials. Based on a number of different experimental procedures, Eimas concluded that the major obstacle to efficient performance for the second graders was a memory deficit. After the second feedback trial, the young subjects would retest hypotheses that had been eliminated from the first feedback trial. With a memory aid, such as leaving the stimuli from the feedback trial in view with a sign to indicate what the feedback had been, the focusing of the second graders improved significantly. This study provides an excellent example of the interdependence between the basic processes of thought. In this instance, a memory deficiency hindered efficient hypothesis testing. Hypothesis generation and testing also overlap considerably with the next process of thought, evaluation.

IV. EVALUATION

In real life it is rarely possible to test a hypothesis completely or even to generate all probable hypotheses. The decision that a hypothesis has been sufficiently tested to accept or reject it plus the strength of one's belief in a hypothesis form the fourth process of thought. Evaluation has been described as "the degree to which the child pauses to consider or assess the quality of his thinking" (Mussen, Conger, & Kagan, 1974, p. 305). Theoretically, if a child offers the very first hypothesis that occurs to him, without evaluating how appropriate or adequate that hypothesis might be, he is not very likely to be correct. If, on the other hand, a child waits until he has thought of several hypotheses and evaluates each one before offering his answer, he is more likely to solve the problem. Kagan has named the first kind of child *impulsive* and the second, *reflective*.

The Matching Familiar Figures test was developed by Kagan to measure reflection-impulsivity (Kagan, Rosman, Day, Albert, & Phillips, 1964). The test consists of sets of line drawings of common objects such as a tree, a pair of scissors, and a baby in a highchair. Each set contains one standard picture and six alternatives. One of the alternatives matches the standard exactly; the other five have some minor change such as a part missing or a straight line changed to a curved line. The child's task is to find the exact match. The time between the presentation of a set of pictures and the child's first guess is the child's latency score; the total number of incorrect guesses made is the child's error score. Most children who are very fast for their age also make many errors and are called impulsive. The children who have long latencies and are fairly accurate are called reflective. Over the years between 5 and 12,

130

children become more reflective (i.e., slower and more accurate).

Kagan has proposed that the most likely reason for a child to be reflective is fear of making a mistake. The reflective child is characterized as being concerned with his performance, and he goes slowly to make sure that he will be correct. The impulsive child, by contrast, is characterized as either not caring at all about his performance or as being more concerned with performing quickly than with being accurate. Although one study (Messer, 1970) is consistent with this theory of the origins of reflection-impulsivity, no study has directly measured the relative anxiety levels of reflective and impulsive children.

Several other theories address the causes of reflection-impulsivity. One currently popular theory proposes that reflective children generate more adequate hypotheses than impulsive children. In terms of the processes of thought considered in this chapter, this theory would shift the determinant for performance on the Matching Familiar Figures test from the evaluation process to the generation of hypotheses process. Support for this position can be found in several studies (Ault, 1973; Denney, 1973; McKinney, Haskins, & Mason, 1974). Ault (1973) and McKinney et al. (1974), for example, both found that impulsive children asked questions on the Twenty Questions game indicative of younger children, whereas reflective children asked more advanced questions. In some studies, impulsive children have been successfully taught strategies for solving the Matching Familiar Figures test (Debus, 1970; Ridberg, Parke, & Hetherington, 1971). These studies are consistent with the theory that impulsive children are deficient in generating and testing hypotheses.

Whether performance on the Matching Familiar Figures test is determined by anxiety, by a deficit in strategy, or by some other factor, we are still faced with a problem. Does the test measure the degree to which a child evaluates his hypotheses before offering them as a response? At the present time we do not have a direct method of assessing how many hypotheses a child thinks about before he responds or how adequately he evaluates each hypothesis. Nevertheless, it is appealing to believe that a process such as evaluation might function at some point during problem-solving. Relative to the other processes considered so far, evaluation has received very little investigation. Consequently it must be regarded, for the moment at least, as a more tentative construct.

One might suppose that the processes of thought operate in the same sequence as they have been presented here: perception, memory, hypothesis generation and testing, and evaluation—a sequence that follows an intuitively logical order. A person ought to perceive a problem before he can generate possible solutions for it, and he ought to generate and test hypotheses before he can evaluate them. However, it is possible that the processes *do not operate sequentially*. Parallel processing is an attractive explanation of why thinking can occur so rapidly, and current theories from the fields of information processing and computer science argue persuasively for *parallel* processing systems.

The interrelationship of the development of the units of thought and the development of the processes of thought is not precisely known, but it is reasonable to assume that there is a correspondence in their changes over time. The functioning of each process affects the development of each unit of thought. Perception, for example, must play a central role in the development of symbols and concepts. Since symbols are arbitrary expressions for schemata, the schemata have to be refined by the perceptual process before symbols could be assigned to them. Likewise, the differentiation of schemata according to their distinctive features permits the development of concepts, since concepts stand for the attributes common to many different events. All of the units of thought are stored in and retrieved from memory; therefore, any limitation of the memory process will necessarily limit the development of the units. The units cannot be enriched, differentiated, made more precise, validated, etc., until the old unit is recalled from memory and the new one replaces it in memory. In a similar manner, as the child generates and tests various hypotheses about the meaning of certain concepts, those concepts might change in status or validity. While it might appear that fairly clear distinctions have been made between each of the units and processes of thought, this appearance is deceptive. Instead of being discrete, the units and processes are interwoven and it is difficult to draw fine lines between them.

In addition to the units and processes of thought, several other variables can influence the likelihood that a child will solve a problem. Among these variables are cultural conditioning, anxiety (e.g., fear of failure), motivation (e.g., desire to succeed, to avoid errors, or to obtain a reward), and expectations for success or failure. All of these factors become more salient with age, but whether they facilitate or impede problem-solving depends on the particular individual. Since these factors are neither general developmental variables nor, strictly speaking, units or processes of thought, we shall not elaborate on them here.

SUMMARY

The process approach to cognitive development has proposed four units and four processes of thought. Several major developmental changes occur in the units of thought. Children shift from a reliance on schemata to the greater use of symbols, concepts, and rules; concepts gain validity, status, and accessibility and are used relatively as well as absolutely; and transformational rules are used in preference to nontransformational rules.

Among the more interesting changes in the development of the perceptual process are increases in the child's attention span, better selectivity of attention, greater speed in shifting attention, and more rapid and more accurate final perceptions. The memory process also changes, with increases in the span of short-term and long-term memory and increased use of rehearsal, imagery, and chunking which facilitate recall. The third process of thought is the generation and testing of hypotheses. As children develop, they generate more adequate and sophisticated hypotheses and then test these hypotheses more systematically (more efficiently). Tasks such as Twenty Questions, probability learning, and Levine's blank trials procedure for the cue-selection problem demonstrate hypothesis generation and testing in both verbal and nonverbal situations. The fourth process of thought, evaluation, is not as clearly understood as the other processes. Kagan developed a test of reflection–impulsivity which he claims measures the degree to which a child pauses to evaluate his hypotheses before offering them. Whether the test actually taps the evaluation process and what variables underlie performance on the test are currently the subject of debate among researchers.

4

A COMPARISON OF APPROACHES

One of the items on a standard intelligence test, such as the Stanford-Binet, asks the 6-year-old child to state one way in which two objects, such as an apple and an orange, are different. At the 7-year-old level, a similarity is asked for, and at the 8-year-old level the child must state both a similarity and a difference. The more similarities and differences a child can state, the brighter (or smarter) he is. Underlying the child's successful responses is the child's knowledge that differences and similarities depend upon the level of analysis. If the focus is on function, both the apple and orange are edible. If the focus is on hierarchical category, both are fruit. The similarities are thus apparent. If, however, the focus shifts to other dimensions, such as perceptual features like color, texture, or taste, then the differences become prominent. The intelligence test recognizes that differences are easier to find than similarities by assigning the question about differences to a younger aged child.

Analogously, we can find both similarities and differences in the two preceding chapters. The differences are more apparent because the framework and terminology of each are very different. In the method of data collection, for example, Piaget primarily observed children, arranging "little tests" only when he believed they would help him distinguish between the child's responses. The tradition of experimental child psychology, on the other hand, has relied heavily on laboratory studies and rigorous scientific procedures. As a consequence of the different methodologies, different organizations have been used to present the data. Piaget's organization has been by stage, starting at birth and proceeding sequentially through childhood, whereas the experimental research has been organized by process, dealing with discrete topics such as perception and memory. Besides making it difficult to compare the process approach to Piaget's theory, the difference in organization represents a fundamental difference in perspective on several related issues.

First, is development regulated by stages such that the sequence of development is fixed? As we noted in the second chapter, development appears to be ordered for some abilities by logical necessity. The ordered development of primary, secondary, and tertiary circular reactions; the stages in the development of object permanence and classification skills; and the sequence of preoperational, concrete operational, and formal operational thinking all seem dictated by the principle that mastery of the previous skill is a prerequisite for the subsequent skill. For other abilities, though, the order in development is apparent only after empirical observation. Thus, the development of conservation of mass before conservation of volume only implies that mass is a simpler concept to learn, not that mass conservation is a subskill of volume conservation. Second, stage theory also implies that there is an ideal end state toward which the child progresses inevitably. (See Figure 4-1.) That is, if development continues at all, its direction is predetermined. Nonstage approaches typically do not carry a similar requirement since environmental forces are given more power to create a diversity of products. Third, adopting a stage orientation presupposes that some behaviors are sufficiently different from previous abilities that we can identify a child as being in or out of a stage. How well that identification can be made depends on the behavior being analyzed.

An appropriate example is contained in language development. The child's level of language development can be characterized by measuring the average sentence length. Before any meaningful words are spoken, the child babbles; then his utterances are only one word long, then two

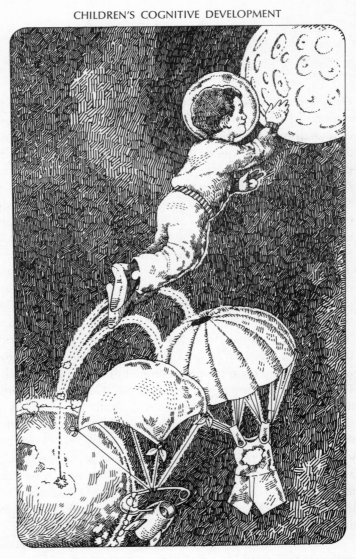

Figure 4-1. An ideal end state in stage theory. Piaget's "stages" of cognitive development pictured as the stages used to launch space craft: (bottom to top) the Sensori-motor and Preoperational stages are jettisoned as the Concrete Operational child follows a trajectory toward the Formal Operational goal.

words long, etc. In learning grammatical rules, there is a time before which the child uses no past tense verbs and after which he does. These observations suggest the presence of stages in language development. Yet, the growth in a child's vocabulary seems better described by a nonstage function. Children add words to their vocabulary incrementally, with no discernible stages. Similarly, the classification of behaviors as preoperational, concrete operational, and formal operational is useful for describing the child's capacity to handle mental operations, and the stage terminology seems appropriate. Stage terminology seems inappropriate to describe the fact that children gradually become more reflective with age, or bring their concepts in line with adult definitions, or become better able to attend selectively.

Even if several aspects of development are suited to a stage conceptualization, they may not follow the same sequence of timing. What we have called Piaget's theory is really many theories on various topics with different stages for each. For example, the stages in the development of object permanence do not correspond perfectly to the stages in the Sensorimotor Period. Whether one chooses a stage theory or not also depends on the level of analysis. If one ignores the day-to-day fluctuations and focuses on a general pattern of behavior that might emerge over months or years, then stage theory may seem more fitting. If day-to-day variability is interesting, then probably no stage theory will fit.

So far in this discussion, the term "stage theory" has been used rather loosely. Actually there is a continuum of positions between two extremes. At one end of the continuum is the view that most of the child's time is spent in one of several stages with short, relatively abrupt transitions between stages. As the length of time spent in a stage is shortened and the time in transition is lengthened, one moves along the continuum until all the time is spent in transition and development is seen as continuous and non-stage. Between these two extremes we can place Piaget's theory and the process approach. To the extent that Piaget's theory is more to the stage end of the continuum, and the process approach is more to the nonstage end, the two are fundamentally different. Moreover, since a nonstage theory does not necessarily dictate any specific end state or single developmental sequence, the study of individual differences assumes more importance in the process approach than in Piaget's theory. We will now briefly examine the treatment of individual differences in each approach.

For the majority of issues presented in this book, development has been described for the normal average child (whoever he might be). Differences between particular individual children have been ignored. In Piaget's theory individual differences were ignored because he was interested in exploring those characteristics of cognitive development that are similar in all children. Piaget sought to describe an ideal process of development, not the daily variations within one child or the differences among children. Nevertheless, Piaget acknowledged individual differences in his methods of assessing children. He believed that if the purpose of testing was to assess what children actually know, then the method of testing must be flexible enough to suit the particular needs of each child. The example of the class inclusion problem in Chapter 2 illustrates the degree to which the tester can try to reshape a problem to elicit the correct answer from the child. Once again, Piaget's methods contrast with the experimental research tradition. The typical procedure for the studies cited in Chapter 3 involves rigid standardization so that each child in any one group receives exactly the same treatment as the other children in that group. While it is rare to report the performance of specific children, individual differences are considered statistically in the range of scores found in each group. Whereas Piaget's method can be criticized for potentially allowing the experimenter to influence the child's responses and thus overestimate what the child knows, the process approach can be criticized for potentially underestimating the child's knowledge because the task was not suited to him.

Nonetheless, both approaches to the study of cognitive

development converge onto the same points, by asking fundamental questions: How does the child think? and What does he think about? Instead of being like the brighter child who tries to list as many similarities and differences as possible, we shall be more selective, highlighting only a few. In this comparison we shall adopt the process organization merely because it is more convenient to bend Piaget's work to focus on processes than the reverse. Whereas Piaget has incorporated each process into his description of stages, the experimental research tradition has, until recently, ignored Piaget's stages and classified children only according to age. Since age of the child does not predict very accurately which Piagetian stage he will be in, it is difficult to fit the process approach to Piaget's theory. Our organization is not intended to convey approval of one approach over the other; rather, it is merely a statement of the relative flexibility of each system. Our comparison begins by pointing out two assumptions which are common to both approaches. Then we will reconsider the topics of concept acquisition, memory, and perception, which play important roles in any discussion of cognitive development.

Most psychologists today consider themselves interactionists, in part because the extreme maturation and learning stances have proven to be untenable. Piaget does lean more toward the maturation side by emphasizing the self-regulatory balance between assimilation and accommodation, whereas the American research tradition has tended to emphasize the environment more. The human organism, even in infancy, is too complex to be described in the relatively simple terms of nativism or empiricism. Although the heredity–environment (nature–nurture; maturation–learning) controversy still arises occasionally in child psychology, the majority position today is that the issue is a false dichotomy. Our research energies can be better spent answering questions other than whether maturation or learning is the more important factor.

The second common assumption is that the child plays an active role in guiding his own development. Unlike a blotter which absorbs ink, a child does not absorb knowledge. Rather, he constructs an interpretation of the information he has selectively attended to, based on his prior experience, his maturation, and his momentary needs, among other factors. The moderate novelty principle plays a key role in determining what the child will learn. This principle states that the child will attend to and learn most from events that are mildly discrepant from his current level of conceptions. In Piaget's terminology, the child will completely assimilate experiences which are identical to previous ones by applying his old schemes without trying to do anything new. If an experience is too discrepant, his old schemes will not be appropriate enough, so he will have no means of coping with the experience, causing him to turn away from it. If the experience is moderately discrepant, however, he can both assimilate and accommodate to it. His old schemes can be applied in part (assimilation) but they are also modified slightly to be more appropriate to the unique aspects of the new experience (accommodation). Under these conditions of accommodation to moderately discrepant events, the child gains the most new knowledge. The same ideas were presented under the topics of attention and perception. A stimulus which is too familiar is boring and results in habituation of attention. A stimulus which is too novel might not contain enough information to be meaningful. A certain amount of redundancy in information is needed, especially for younger children, to make sense of perceptual input.

SIMILARITIES IN TOPICS

Concept Acquisition

Piaget has made extensive observations of children's acquisitions of the concepts of space, time, and causality (Piaget, 1929; 1930). For example, children believe nighttime comes so that people can sleep, that the moon blows away the sun to allow the night to come, and that God (or Mother) makes it dark at night by telling the sun to go away. Not only are the child's beliefs amusing, but they also demonstrate his lack of awareness of physical cause-and-effect. Another way of putting this is that the concept of night lacks status and validity. The fascination with children's attributions of causality continues. Bernstein and Cowan (1975) recently asked children from 3 to 12 years old to explain how people get babies. Cabbage patches and storks have been replaced by baby stores and hospitals, but the explanations still remain fanciful.

The mistakes that children make while they acquire concepts are frequently humorous to adults, yet concept acquisition is serious work for the child. In fact, concept acquisition lies at the heart of cognitive development because children must master conceptual relationships before they can use these relationships in abstract thinking. The world is too complex, it contains too much information, for a person to deal with each piece of information separately. To be able to handle the enormous amount of available information, we must be able to organize the information into patterns, classify the patterns into groups, and arrange those groups into higher order patterns. Piaget's term, *organization*, describes this information-reducing ability. So does the term, *rule-making*, for rules are simply the formulas which codify the raw information. Since rules specify a relationship between concepts, concept acquisition is of utmost importance in abstract thinking.

We have already examined these ideas in our previous discussion of *intension*. The intension of a class or of a concept is simply the rule which defines what elements belong appropriately in that class or concept.* Once we know the intension of a class, we can decide if a novel object belongs to that class. If it does, we can respond to it as we would respond to any other member of the class. Thus, we do not need to remember a huge number of responses to a huge number of different stimuli. We only need remember a more limited set of responses and have an organizational scheme (or conceptual framework, or classification procedure) for deciding the class to which the new stimulus belongs. This same principle of organization applies to chunking, which eases memory load.

Children's ability to classify objects has been studied with Piaget's multiple classification and class inclusion (part–whole) tasks. We can also study the extent to which a child's use of a concept matches some adult standard for that concept (its status, validity, etc.) and how a child uses concepts or classification to solve problems (e.g., the Twenty Questions game). Although the congruence between word usage and conceptual knowledge is certainly not perfect, we can examine a child's use of words, particularly as he is learning to speak fluently, for an insight into his knowledge of concepts.

Take the ostensibly simple situation of acquiring vocabulary. Parents, or other friendly adults, point to something or touch it and utter some sounds, such as "table." Then they point to and label "doggie" and "daddy." The

---

* A *class* is defined as any collection of objects which bear a common feature, whereas a *concept* is "a generalized idea of a class of objects based on knowledge of particular instances of the class" (*Webster's New World Dictionary*, 1960).

same point-and-label game is played many times in a day, over many days and often across many different instances of the object (e.g., different dogs and different tables are indicated) until the child seems to be using those words correctly. Then the child sees some novel things, perhaps a different breed of dog, a cat, a differently shaped table, and an unfamiliar man. The child correctly labels the table and the dog. He also calls the cat "doggie" and the man "daddy." The child almost certainly can perceive physical differences between the cat and the dog, and between the stranger and his father, but he has to determine if those differences are important ones. Should the cat be called something totally different from the dog or is it just a minor variation, like the minor differences between a collie and a shepherd? From the child's perspective, what is the difference between daddy and any other man? If it is important that one person takes care of him and the other does not, then why are "mommy" and "daddy" called by two different names? They both take care of him. Somewhere in language learning, the child has to figure out which attributes or features of an object are critical for meeting the definitional requirements and which are extraneous or irrelevant. When a child generalizes inappropriately and calls a cat "doggie," we can infer that some of the features that both animals have in common are included in the child's concept relating to that word. By calling a strange man "daddy," the child reveals that he was attending to adult male features and that he had assumed "daddy" was a class name rather than a proper name for one particular element of that class. Greenfield (1973) has documented how her child apparently focused on the features of caretaker when learning "daddy." Her child called three people (mother, father, and babysitter) by that one name. Similarly, we can guess that a child who says "up" for wanting either to be picked up or to be put down has a concept of "changing position from where I am now." That concept is not represented by a single word in the adult language.

The immensity of the child's task in learning vocabulary words seems even more incredible when one considers that a dimension which is important for distinguishing between two classes of objects may be irrelevant for distinguishing between two others. For adults, one relevant difference between cats and dogs is what noise each animal makes, but size and color are irrelevant. From the child's point of view, there is nothing so special about noise that it should serve as a definitional feature while size and color differences are ignored. Then, when the child learns the difference between trees and shrubs, he has to pay attention to size, instead of color or noise; and the most reliable cue for distinguishing between ambulances and police cars is color, rather than size or noise. Thus, when we credit a child with the ability to label an object correctly, we can also credit him with considerable knowledge about the class to which that object belongs.

Because the development of concepts plays such a central role in cognitive development, it would be strange indeed if both the theory of Piaget and the process approach did not each investigate conceptual development. Similarly, because the child must learn to use his memory efficiently, the construction of internal representations is another important topic that the study of cognitive development must investigate.

In the third chapter, we presented one method for organizing a discussion of memory. Memory was divided into three parts, sensory, short-term, and long-term, as a function of how long information would remain in that store. A distinction was drawn between recall tasks and recognition tasks which tap different degrees to which one "has" a memory. Imagery, rehearsal, and chunking were some of the deliberate strategies for increasing the probability that an item would be remembered.

That discussion focused on "how" questions: How long can we remember an item? How do we test for the presence of a memory? How do we put items into memory? We could, instead, focus on a "what" question: What do we remember? One answer is that we remember the units of thought: schemata, symbols, concepts, and rules. Evidence for schemata was obtained from the habituation phenomenon and demonstrates memory in very young infants. Piaget agrees that young infants have memories. Part of the increasing proficiency of reflexive responses in the very first stage of the Sensorimotor Period comes when the infant recognizes, at least in a rudimentary fashion, that he has encountered the stimulus before and has previously accommodated to it. Similarly, the development of object permanence shows the memory capacity of the infant.

The schema, which is the primary form of memory for a child in the Sensorimotor Period, incorporates the various aspects of the sensations and motor movements associated with some activity (Elkind, 1967a). The infant remembers his rattle as some combination of the tactile sensations from grasping it, the auditory sensations from its sound when shaken, visual sensations such as its color, and the grasping and shaking movements. These movements are

151

what Piaget has called schemes, organized patterns of behavior.* Thus, in the Sensorimotor Period, schemata are closely linked to schemes in the sense that the infant's schemata are representations of schemes as well as sensations. Although the older child and adult acquire additional memories for symbols, concepts, and rules, schemata continue to be used and remembered. Adults give up riding bicycles in favor of driving cars and may not have been on ice skates since they were children, but they can call on their riding and skating skills many years later when their own children ask to be taught them. The schemata retained from the childhood experiences save the parent from embarrassing if not fatal accidents on the bike or skates. Since schemata also play an important role in Piaget's theory of perception, let us consider that topic as a final issue in this chapter.

Perception

Piaget has suggested a theory of perception, but it is less complete and less accessible to the reader than his theory of cognitive development. Gibson (1969) has classified Piaget's theory of perception as an enrichment theory because information from schemata are added to the basic sensory data through the process of assimilation and the schemata, in turn, are modified to accommodate the specific stimulus input. The characterization of Piaget's theory as an enrichment theory focuses attention on the schemata that become enriched. Piaget's theory has an additional focus, however, on the development of certain mental opera-

---

* The unfortunate similarity of the words *scheme* and *schema* still plagues us. Recall that a scheme (plural: schemes) is an organized pattern of behavior and a schema (plural: schemata) is an elementary memory.

tions, similar to cognitive operations, that influence perception (Elkind, 1975). Those operations are *perceptual regulations* which give the child new methods of manipulating perceptual data mentally. At first the child's perceptions are centered on a few aspects of the stimulus which are highly salient and which capture his attention. The stimulus controls the child's attention, so his attention is stimulus bound. According to Piaget, the development of perceptual regulations free the child's attention, allowing him to choose and control where he directs his attention. In other words, perception becomes decentered through the operation of perceptual regulations. The change from centering to decentering is directly analogous to the improvements in selective attention discussed under the process approach.

To make these ideas clearer, we can consider two abilities that arise from the development of perceptual regulations. One of them involves mentally rearranging a stimulus event by combining or separating various aspects of it to create a new perception. Some visual stimuli, for example, can be viewed as two different figures, depending on which areas are seen as central to a figure and which as the background. The young child centers on only one organization and perceives a single figure. The older child is able to decenter and reorganize the stimulus to perceive both figures. Piaget attributes the ability to reorganize the picture to perceptual regulations which allow the child to add or subtract areas and contours from the picture to form all the possible figures and their corresponding backgrounds. This is illustrated in Figure 4-2, which is perceived as a vase if the black area is considered the central figure, and the entire image minus the black area the background. The picture is perceived as two faces if the entire image minus the black area is considered the central figure, taking the black area as the background.

Figure 4-2. An ambiguous figure with two perceptual organizations.

The other perceptual ability involves part–whole perception. To test this, a child is shown a set of pictures in which one familiar object is constructed using other familiar objects as parts. For example, a man can be made up of pieces of fruit, with bananas representing the man's legs and a pear representing his body. Children who have not yet acquired the necessary perceptual regulations will center only on the parts and report seeing the fruit or on the whole and report seeing the man. Children who have the perceptual regulations, however, can decenter and see both the parts and the whole simultaneously, reporting a man made up of fruit. These perceptual regulations are analogous to the cognitive operations used in the part–whole cognitive task described in the class inclusion problem. In both, the child must consider simultaneously more than one facet of the problem or stimulus.

SUMMARY

Both differences and similarities can be found between the Piagetian and the process approaches to cognitive development. One major difference stems from Piaget's theory incorporating the concept of stages whereas the process approach does not. Four questions can be raised in pursuing the stage versus nonstage issue: (a) Is the sequence of development fixed? (b) Is there an ideal end state toward which development proceeds? (c) Can a child be assessed as being in or out of a stage? and (d) What level of analysis (day-to-day variability or larger time blocks) is used? A second distinction between the two approaches is apparent in their consideration of individual differences. Piaget's research has allowed for individual differences by using flexible testing procedures. The process approach has used standardized test situations but included estimates of individual differences in statistical summaries of the data.

In spite of these differences, both approaches agree on two basic assumptions: that development results from an interaction between biological and environmental forces and that the child plays an active role in regulating his own development. In addition, each approach has investigated many common topics, including concept acquisition, memory, and perception. Concept acquisition is critical in any theory of cognitive development because concepts permit the efficient handling of enormous amounts of information. Although the relationship between language and conceptual development is imperfect, language provides one measure of the child's knowledge of concepts. Because concepts and the other units of thought are stored in and retrieved from memory, the memory process must also be investigated to build a picture of cognitive development. Schemata, the first kind of mental representation available to the infant, were re-examined, particularly in terms of their incorporation of sensorimotor schemes. Finally, Piaget's theory of perception was characterized as an enrichment theory but with an additional focus on perceptual regulations that enable the child's perceptions to become decentered.

5

IMPLICATIONS FOR PARENTS AND TEACHERS

PARENTING IMPLICATIONS

Since the focus of this book has been on cognitive development rather than socialization, this section on parenting will not discuss such traditional parenting concerns as toilet training and sibling rivalry. Instead, we hope to convey a sense of how to enjoy children by watching their cognitive development. While most grandparents expect to receive news when their grandchild sits up alone, cuts his first tooth, and crawls, they do not expect letters containing such milestones as coordinating secondary reactions or searching for hidden objects. Although these cognitive achievements are more difficult to observe, they can be just as exciting and rewarding for the parent and grandparent. Besides being fun, we hope the focus on cognitive development will present alternative interpretations for some potentially irritating child behaviors. Recall the example from Piaget's fifth stage in the Sensorimotor Period in which the child repeatedly drops toys out of his playpen. While one could easily think that the child was maliciously attempting to annoy his mother, the alternative explanation offered here was that the dropping activity was essential practice of tertiary circular reactions.

The material in this section is organized around the broad age groups of infants, preschoolers, elementary school children, and adolescents. This is convenient because parents and other adults use age as a reference marker, to judge whether a child is acting "normally" and to know what behavior or level of performance to expect from him. This is not meant to deny the individual differences between children. Rather, it just reminds us that children are perceived both as individuals and as members of an age group. This same distinction is made by parents in judging their children's actions. When their child is behaving nicely, parents offer the explanation that their love and gentle guidance produced a well-mannered child. When their child misbehaves, he is "going through a stage" or "acting like all the other two-year-olds" (or 10-year-olds or adolescents).

One of the major themes of this section is that enjoyment is produced by solving challenging cognitive tasks, and frustration is produced when the task proves too difficult. For the child, challenging cognitive tasks confront him every day. He has to figure out how his world functions. For the parent, the challenging task is figuring out how the child functions. The purpose of this section is to illuminate the parent's task.

Infancy

Everyone knows that babies enjoy playing peek-a-boo. For many adults, it is sufficient to know that baby can be amused temporarily by playing this game. To understand why the baby enjoys it, we can examine the development of objective permanence. It is a cognitive challenge for the infant to figure out that objects can hide temporarily and then reappear. When such an interesting object as his mother hides and reappears, often with a smiling or playful expression on her face, he has an opportunity to exercise his ideas of object permanence. Since her appearance and disappearance are fairly regular in the game context, it is an excellent opportunity for him to verify her object permanence and to enjoy solving this problem.

The development of object permanence can also explain situations of distress for the infant. Consider the situation where the infant has been playing happily by himself. Suddenly he begins to cry. The toy that he had held in his hand is on the floor behind him. If this child is younger than six or seven months, one might correctly suspect that his crying resulted from frustration at not being able to find the "hidden" toy. Returning the toy to his line of vision will bring instant relief. The development of objective permanence can also be related to separation anxiety. The expression of separation anxiety, only too familiar to parents, is intense distress when parents leave their infant, especially in an unfamiliar room or with an unfamiliar person. There are many instances when the infant does not seem to differentiate between his mother's leaving the living room to go to the kitchen and her leaving him in the capable hands of a babysitter. He still wails at the separation. People, being like objects to the infant, acquire a permanence of existence, so he becomes upset when they disappear and he cannot find them or make them reappear.

As soon as the infant leaves the immobility of his first few months and begins to creep, crawl, or walk, literally a whole new world becomes available to him. Prior to self-initiated traveling, the infant's world is severely limited to those objects his parents bring close to him. After he can navigate around the house or yard, and in spite of his parents' best efforts to baby-proof the environment, he will undoubtedly get into something dangerous or forbidden. As a result, he is required to learn distinctions between permissible and forbidden activities. The difficulty for the infant is that similar actions do not bring similar parental responses.

Parents generally believe that baby grasping his doll or mother's finger is cute; baby grasping a knife, however, is dangerous. Baby reaching for his bottle will get smiles of encouragement; baby reaching for a full glass will get scolded. Baby pulling on a string attached to a toy is playing; baby pulling on a cord attached to a lamp is in trouble. From the parents' perspective, their baby is alternately angelic and mischievous. From the baby's perspective, his parents are alternately benevolent and malevolent. Certainly parents must teach their children which activities are permitted and which are not. They should not be surprised, however, that the discriminations are difficult ones for their child to make. Piaget suggested that the first classification of objects is made according to what schemes can be applied to them. Lamp cords and toy cords are both objects to be pulled, so the child classifies them together. By forbidding the pulling of lamp cords and permitting the pulling of toy cords, parents require their child to reclassify the objects along a different dimension. The more dimensions of difference between the permitted and forbidden activity, the more likely the child will find one that allows him to avoid the activity his parents disapprove of. Even then, he might make the discrimination on an incorrect basis. For example, if he decides that lamp cords are forbidden because they are brown in color whereas toy cords are permissibly white, he will successfully avoid pulling on the lamp until his parents purchase a new lamp with a white cord. Parents then will wonder why their child is suddenly naughty again, and the child will wonder what went wrong.

The Preschool Years

A three-year-old drags his mother to the kitchen, opens the oven door, places his hands inside, brings them out again, and extends his arm toward his mother. Smiling, he says, "Want a cookie, Mommy?" There is nothing in his hand. During the Preoperational Period, especially in the pre-school years from three to five, children engage in a considerable amount of fantasy play. The world of make-believe is made possible because the Preoperational child has acquired the ability to use symbols. Symbols and language free the child's thinking from the immediately perceptible and permit the child to create thoughts out of his imagination.

It is not the child's vivid imagination, however, that leads him to complain about his share of dinner or dessert. If his sibling's piece of pie is shorter but wider than his own, he is likely to believe he got shortchanged. Without a notion of compensation, the nonconserving preschooler will not accept his parents' explanations of equality. Moreover, research on teaching conservation warns parents that they will not be able to teach conservation concepts very easily.

Parents of prechoolers should have realistic expectations for the kinds of stories their children can tell. Anyone who has tried to piece together a preschooler's description of his daily activities will recognize the egocentric aspects of his speech. He starts his tale in the middle (if not at the end) and leaves out essential bits of information because he fails to take the perspective of the listener into account. Ambiguous references as in "and then he took his and gave it to her to stop her crying" make sense to the speaker because he knows that Johnny took his paintbrush ("he took his") and gave it to Mary ("her") who had cried because a third child had grabbed Mary's paintbrush. That the tale does not make sense to the adult merely weakens the child's faith in the omniscience of parents.

The distortions that can occur as the young child tries to make sense of a newly encountered experience can be understood in the context of the terms *assimilation* and *accommodation.* For example, Bernstein and Cowan (1975) reported on children's explanations of where babies come from. One child said, "They just get a duck or a goose and they get a little more growned . . . and then they, turn into a baby . . . they give them some food, people food, and they grow like a baby" (p. 87). A book read to that child about animal and human reproduction was probably too complex for the child to understand. He assimilated the information about babies into terms he was more familiar with: ducks hatching from eggs and feeding people to help them grow. Grandmother's advice to explain events in a child's own language is, indeed, sage. When more information than the child can handle is provided, at best, it is ignored and, at worst, completely distorted.

Before parents can answer the preschooler's questions, they must figure out what he asked. That is not as easy as it might appear, as we are reminded by the familiar joke about a child who asked where he came from. After receiving a long explanation about human reproduction from an embarrassed parent, he said, "But Johnny comes from Ohio, where do I come from?" Elkind (1974) has suggested that young children tend to ask questions about psychological causality although the inquiries might appear to concern physical causes. A typical four-year-old might ask "Why is the grass green?" or "Why do birds sing?" The answers that satisfy the preschooler involve psychological interpretations: the grass is green so it will look pretty; birds sing because they are happy.

What else can parents of a preschooler expect? Based on

his memory capacity, he should not always be expected to remember what he has been asked to do. On his way to fetching father's slippers he might get distracted by a toy. Face and hands might be washed, but ears forgotten, if the list of things to wash is too long. The apparent disadvantage of the preschooler's immature memory is offset because he also might forget some treat that had been promised him by a harried parent. Thus, his short memory span may create frustration when parents want him to concentrate on a task, but he is easily distracted from a forbidden activity by the offer of an equally attractive, permitted activity.

Although the preschooler's perceptions lead him to believe that his closet becomes a monster as soon as the bedroom light is turned off, his perceptions also allow him to enjoy the fantasy of cartoons and fairy tales. Thus, the young child's limited cognitive capacities make him as lovable in one context as he is devilish in another.

The Elementary School Years

To many observers, the elementary school years are relatively quiet ones. Before school starts each day, parents usually see a routine of washing, dressing, and eating breakfast. After school and a quick snack, the children are off to play. Perhaps after dinner, some time is spent doing homework, practicing a music lesson, or watching TV. Occasionally, a game or two is played. Minor skirmishes may be fought among siblings about who gets to pick the next TV show or who has to bathe first that evening, but in general the children do not need to be monitored like younger children do. Since playing games absorbs much time during these elementary school years, let us focus more closely on the impact of cognitive development on games.

For many parents, sending their children "off to play"

means some period of relatively undisturbed quiet for them. They presume that children enjoy themselves, learn something about cooperating and competing with peers, and, if nothing else, exercise their bodies to discharge excess energy. (It is considered excess only because children seem to have more energy than parents.) Without denying these benefits of play, children also exercise their minds while playing games.

We have already seen that the game of Twenty Questions exercises children's skills of hypothesis testing. Card games provide practice with numbers and with classification skills. In gin rummy, for example, a number (e.g., 6) can be part of a run (5, 6, 7, and 8) or it can be part of a set of 6's, one from each suit. The child who keeps both possibilities in mind simultaneously will do better than the child who fixes on one plan and ignores the other. Memory is also important as the child tries to keep track of what discards have been made, and how these affect some possible plays in his own hand. He can also develop hypotheses about which cards are likely to benefit his opponent, and arithmetic skills are practiced in calculating the score. When adults play with children, they notice a trial-and-error approach to games which seems haphazard or scatter-brained, and frequently the child exhibits an unwarranted satisfaction with the one hypothesis he generated instead of a thoughtful consideration of many alternative solutions. These methods of solving problems seem more reasonable when put in the context of concrete operational thinking, the most likely period of development for the elementary school aged child.

When there are several different strategies for solving a task, children of a wide variety of ages can enjoy the game (although the older child or adult with multiple strategies is likely to do better). Consider a children's party game of rearranging a set of letters to form as many words as possible. One strategy is to think of a word and then see if the available letters will spell it. Another strategy is to pick several letters at random and try combining them in several orders, then return those letters to the entire array and randomly choose another subset. A third strategy is to search for those letter combinations which are more likely to be found in the language as root words. Although these strategies differ considerably in their sophistication and probability for success, even young elementary schoolers can play the game and see it as a challenge to their problem-solving skills.

With the possibility of analyzing their children's strategies, it is likely to occur to parents that they could try to teach their children the more advanced strategies.* Two questions should be raised: Can they teach the strategies? and Should they teach the strategies? The first is an empirical question. Depending upon the parents' ability to analyze the child's current level of functioning and to teach the more advanced strategies in a way that is meaningful to the child, some parents will experience considerably more success than others. The second question is a philosophical one. Like many educational practices, there is a cost-benefit ratio. The costs are in time and motivation. If the child is led to believe that his way of playing a game is wrong or stupid, and if he experiences any difficulty in learning the correct or smart way, he is simply likely to avoid playing. It will cease to be fun for him. If, on the other hand, he learns relatively quickly and painlessly, the rewards may be self-satisfaction in solving a problem in a new manner or the competitive advantage of knowing a better way to play. Obviously there can be no hard-and-

---

* Indeed, the search for training programs that accelerate children's acquisition of a particular skill seems to be a preoccupation among American researchers and educators. Piaget has found this theme to recur so often that he labels it "The American Question."

fast rule about whether to teach children different ways to play such games. The examples are offered here for the purpose of explaining some aspects of children's behavior that are not often examined. Whether parents choose to observe in quiet fascination or to intervene actively by trying to instruct is a choice that cannot be made without knowing the particulars of the situation: the particular game, the particular child, his level of functioning, the particular set of parents, etc.

Adolescence

Finally, we come to consider parenting the adolescent. We have already seen that the Formal Operational adolescent is likely to appear argumentative and perpetually dissatisfied with parental solutions as he examines his old belief sets and discovers their inconsistencies. Profound shock awaits the unsuspecting parents who suddenly confront a lanky teenager who is asking why . . . why he cannot enjoy drinking, smoking, or sex; why he has to attend religious services; even why he has to attend school. These *why* questions are much different from the four-year-old's. The psychological interpretations that satisfy the preschooler are obviously not going to please the adolescent. He needs detailed, factual explanations, often including rationalizations, for why he must engage in a particular behavior when adults are not required to do so. Parents should expect charges of hypocrisy if their responses to the adolescent are not satisfactory.

Parents may protest that no answer ever seems satisfactory for their adolescent. Several options are available: (a) parents can explore whether there was a hidden question underlying the verbalized one and also attempt to answer it; (b) parents can try to assess if their manner of answering so challenged the adolescent that he denied the validity of their response in order not to appear stupid or silly; (c) parents can ask their adolescent to offer and then criticize his own answers, so parents are put in the position of being a sounding board rather than an answering service; and (d) parents can admit that the answer that satisfies them may not satisfy him, but they seek cooperation with certain rules anyway. A few additional comments need to be made pertaining to the third suggestion of reflecting back the adolescent's concerns without explicitly answering his questions. This technique is common in certain types of psychotherapies (e.g., Rogerian) and in newspaper advice columns (e.g., Ginot's work). It is easy to implement,* but it can also become too automatic, overused, and unsatisfactory when the adolescent truly seeks his parents' opinions.

Advice on parenting is difficult to give and difficult to receive. This section has offered suggestions for analyzing various problem situations and recommended that parents create their own list of solutions. The explanation that a child drops food from his highchair because of circular reactions is not advice on how to cope with that situation. Some mothers will spread a plastic sheet over the floor and let the child drop as much as he pleases. Other mothers will feed the child, denying him access to the food. Still others will ask the child to make a distinction between dropping toys, which is an acceptable activity, and dropping food, which is not. There is no one right method of parenting. Instead, for any one problem there is a variety of potential solutions. Although these change as the child develops, one hopes that there will always be at least one

---

* Its ease of use has been demonstrated with a dialogue between human subjects and a computer program called ELIZA that convincingly simulates a psychiatrist's response to a patient's statements (Weizenbaum, 1968).

solution that is acceptable both to parent and to child. The only advice a book such as this can give is to recommend that parents weigh such factors as the child's current level of development, his motivation to change, the importance of the task demanded of him, the amount of time available for change, and the acceptability of restructuring the task.

There are occasions when a careful weighing of these factors leads to no resolution of the conflict at all. For example, the child might not be capable of making the response his parents require, but they are unwilling to drop their demands. Then advice-giving is futile. One such episode occurred when a father asked me how to stop his two-year-old daughter from eating cigarettes. I asked him to analyze the situation from her perspective.* First, she watches him put cigarettes into his mouth. Imitation is a highly probable response, especially considering her age. Since she has no experience with smoking, she probably assimilates the activity she sees into the more familiar eating scheme. The problem her father would like her to solve is a discrimination between his smoking, which she should not imitate, and his eating, which she should. That distinction might have been beyond her capability. Secondly, the cigarettes are easily accessible on the coffee table. Because they are rather novel, she has a high motivation to investigate them, including shredding them and tasting them. Furthermore, she is allowed to pull apart and taste other items, especially foods, that are given her from the same coffee table. Again, the discrimination asked of her is a difficult one.

My advice to the father was to keep his cigarettes out of reach. Then if he would wait a few years, she would be more easily able to make the required distinctions between smoking and eating, and between eating food and eating

* I stifled my initial reaction which was to tell him to stop bringing cigarettes into the home.

170

cigarettes. The father, unfortunately, found it too big an imposition to change his own habits regarding where he kept his cigarettes, and he did not believe that his daughter might be too immature (both cognitively and emotionally) to learn the task that he had created. I predicted frustration for him and his child and resolved to limit my advice-giving to those really willing to take it.

EDUCATIONAL IMPLICATIONS

The Process Approach

When several different psychological perspectives all advocate the same educational practice, the recommendations can take on an air of being common-sense. They appear obvious and one wonders why anyone bothered to state them. Some, if not all, of the following statements may appear obvious to the reader, but the statements need to be made explicitly because they remind the educator where to look when difficulties arise in the educational process.

It is, for example, a truism that the child must direct his attention to the important aspects of a problem before he can begin to solve it. When a child is not successful in his attempts to solve a problem, his teacher can examine the task to see what demands it makes on his attention. Perhaps some aspects of it are so compelling that he cannot attend to the relevant features. Or, alternatively, the entire task may be so uncompelling as not to attract enough attention. Consider a book aimed at teaching the young child to read. If the different letters in a word are printed in bright colors, the child might not attend sufficiently to the shapes of the letters which distinguish them. If there are interesting pictures opposite the print, the child might prefer to look at the pictures. On the other hand, with no pictures or colors, the child may not be attracted to the book at all.

Similarly, it is obvious that both perception and memory play a role in reading. The reader must perceive the subtle distinctions between letters and the different sized spaces between letters and between words. He must also control the direction of his visual scan so that words are not read backwards (e.g., "saw" for "was"). Learning to scan a page in the proper direction is sufficiently challenging that children practice it spontaneously until it is mastered. Elkind and Weiss (1967) demonstrated this when they asked children to name pictures that were arranged in a triangle. Five-year-old and eight-year-old children read the pictures by starting at the top and following around the triangular outline. Many of the young readers (six and seven years old) read the pictures from left to right and top to bottom. This was clearly a less efficient scanning strategy that was applied inappropriately, but it provided practice on a skill that was being learned. Teachers should always be alert to the possibility that poor performance on one task may result from the child's spontaneous practice of an unrelated or even competing skill.

Memory is called on in reading to figure out what words are spelled by the individual letters and to recall the first words in the sentence as the last words are being read. When a new word is encountered, the child can try to guess its meaning from the context. This involves hypothesis generation and testing, with the generated hypotheses being a function of the child's prior experiences. It is not uncommon for the beginning reader to encounter the following passage, "The dog said woof-woof," and read instead, "The dog said arf-arf," because his prior experience with dogs supplied an incorrect guess about the last word. Another intrusion of prior experience into reading occurred when the young son of a physician laughed and said, "There's a doctor named Ugs." The sign he had read was "Drugs," but he had interpreted it as "Dr. Ugs" in keeping with his familiarity with doctors.

Educators would also consider it obvious that children cannot be expected to learn complex responses until they have mastered the more simple components. Single digit addition is, therefore, taught before multiple digit addition, and both are well learned before multiplication and division are attempted. One can forget, however, that children might be able to solve some simple problems but still not know the general rule governing the process. One child announced to his astonished math teacher that he knew when numbers were odd or even only up to three digit numbers. It was frightening to think that he must have memorized which of 999 numbers were odd and which were even, when all he needed to learn was the oddness—evenness of the digits 0 through 9 and a rule to examine only the last digit of the number.

A child might have difficulty learning if some concepts are too abstract, too complex, or lack status or validity. When the child's sense of time is not fully developed, he will have as much trouble conceptualizing ancient Roman battles as the last World War. His teacher may have vivid personal memories of the latter, but to the child, both are equally foreign and distant. The succession of English kings or American presidents are lists to be learned by rote, since the child has no personal experience with either kings or presidents. In fact, younger children's concepts of political systems and government are personalized, concrete, and incomplete (Adelson & O'Neil, 1966). When asked the function of taxes, for example, 11-year-olds might reply, "to pay for the police," whereas the 18-year-old might answer, "to run the entire government." The younger child's answer deals with a highly visible service, one that he is quite familiar with. The adolescent can refer to less visible, more abstract functions and knows that there is more to government than just police and firemen.

The general principle advocated here is that teachers should examine their curriculum material to see if it is suited to their pupils' current abilities. With the gross national product and the yearly government budget mind-boggling to adults, it is no wonder that economics is not taught in elementary school. When a lesson is not being learned well, it can be analyzed in terms of the demands it makes on the students' thought processes. The teacher might need to explain a fundamental concept or rule upon which the lesson is built, or change the lesson to draw the child's attention to the relevant aspects, or help the student recall critical pieces of information, or help him generate and test hypotheses. The reader is reminded of some previously discussed research which bears directly on this issue. Gelman (1969), for example, showed how attracting the child's attention to the relevant aspects of a situation improved performance on a conservation task. In Eimas's (1970) study, memory aids helped children solve a cue selection problem. More sophisticated and efficient hypotheses were generated in a Twenty Questions game when the pictures were ordered according to conceptual categories (Ault, 1973; Van Horn & Bartz, 1968). In essence, there are many factors influencing learning, and the failure of any one of them might cause failure to learn the lesson.

The Piagetian Approach

Since many experiments on cognitive development were purposely constructed to resemble academic tasks, it seems obvious that teachers can analyze their lesson plans in terms of the processes of thought. It is not as obvious how Piaget's theory can be applied to a classroom situation. Piaget was not particularly interested in translating his psychological ideas into educational practices. The research effort stimulated by his theory was, at first, likewise geared toward substantiating or refuting his observations on cognitive development. Consequently, it has only been in the past few years that Piagetian-based classrooms have been organized. There has not yet been enough time to evaluate these experimental classrooms, so we shall discuss instead the general implications for a classroom of adopting Piaget's theory, rather than report any specific curriculum suggestions. The examples that follow are drawn primarily from preschool situations, but the principles they illustrate apply equally to other age groups.

Two very different aspects of Piaget's theory have gained recognition in educational circles. One is an attraction with the conservation task and the desire to teach it to children in the Preoperational Period. If the teaching is attempted out of the belief that all cognitive development will thus be hastened, then this belief is incorrect. Achieving conservation is not the goal of development. Rather, the goal is to form the mental structures (through both maturation and experience) that normally enable the child to exhibit conservation. Conservation is a necessary by-product of the development of concrete operations; it is not the development itself. According to Piaget, providing the prior experience but not allowing time for physical growth will do no more than teach the child a very specific response to a very specific stimulus. The underlying mental structures will not have changed, so no general, useful learning will have occurred. In addition, learning takes time. If we try to teach a child something too early, it will simply take more time than if we wait until he is ready. The difference in the two lengths of time is the time we cannot spend teaching him other things. Before devising ever more clever teaching gimmicks, we ought to consider the costs and benefits to the child of learning that particular skill at that particular time rather than at another time.

Piaget's emphasis on maturation is, once again, readily apparent, and that is the second aspect of his system to capture the interest of educators. It recalls the familiar notion of readiness to learn and appears to advocate not forcing a child to learn anything he does not seem interested

176

in learning. To many, it seems a fairly pessimistic view of what educators can or should do. It seems one must wait around until the child mysteriously grows; then one must keep a sharp watch for the child's signal that he is ready to learn. An emphasis on maturation need not, however, embody a pessimism about teaching. Maria Montessori's educational philosophy is both strongly maturational and not pessimistic. Piaget has frequently been compared to Montessori (Elkind, 1967b), so readers already familiar with her system of education will recognize many of the following ideas.

Piaget and Montessori

Usually, theories that stress maturation also advocate that children have an intrinsic motivation to learn. That is, the impetus for development is internal. Piaget and Montessori agree that children are curious about their world and continually seek to understand it. In the Sensorimotor and Preoperational Periods, such curiosity is displayed by children's active manipulation of objects. In later periods, curiosity is evident in their questions about daily events, school work, world news, and so forth. Education can help the child satisfy his curiosity by providing experiences which suit his level of development. For the preschool child this means that he should be given tasks that allow him to act on objects. To learn about numbers, he should have things to count. Objects should be provided for him to touch or move as he repeats a number aloud. He can be given dolls and houses to place in one-to-one correspondence or he can set as many places for lunch as there are children in the classroom.

To learn about colors, the child might sort colored objects, not just recite names while a teacher holds up a colored swatch. To learn shapes, he can place shapes in a form board, copy specific designs, or walk a pattern on the floor. The essential aspects are movement and acting on objects. Verbal abstractions are minimized for two reasons: they do not capture the child's attention very well and they are not active enough or concrete enough to produce learning, given the mental structures available at that level of development. Moreover, Piaget believes that the young child's language facility lags behind his cognitive development, so teaching him cognitive skills using his weaker verbal skills is not likely to be efficient.

If children already have an interest in learning, then it is the teacher's obligation to foster that interest and make sure that it does not get stifled. The teacher can provide a wide variety of activities so that children do not become bored. She must also make sure that enough familiar activities occur so children have some old experiences to tie new experiences to. These recommendations coincide with Piaget's assimilation and accommodation principles, but they are also widely accepted practices advocated in nearly all educational systems.

Another point of similarity between Piaget and Montessori is the emphasis each has placed on development being ordered in stages. For Montessori, this has meant that learning activities are programmed in a particular sequence that all children must follow. As we have already noted, in a very general sense learning must be sequenced from simpler to more complex skills. Algebra and chemistry are taught as formal operational skills develop. Counting is taught before addition; multiple classification develops before hierarchical ordering. Just how far the notion of sequencing must be carried, however, is open to question. Montessori recommends a fixed sequence of activities. Piaget's writings are unclear on this point, so it is likely that different educators will interpret his work in different ways.

Contrary to Montessori, it may be that no one sequence of learning suits every child because each child brings a different set of prior experiences with him to the task. A more flexible approach would allow the child the freedom to order his own learning. Of course, it is necessary to trust that the child contains the mechanisms to regulate his own learning. The obligation of teachers is to make sure that the child has confidence in himself and is free from criticism so that he will venture into learning activities.

Two other aspects of children's learning, important to both Montessori and Piaget, are imitation and repetition. The function of repetition in learning is to practice actions or strategies that are not fully efficient. Just as physical movements need practice to operate smoothly and rapidly, cognitive actions need practice. Piaget noted the repetitions that defined the primary, secondary, and tertiary circular reaction stages in the Sensorimotor Period. Although repetitions do not define later stages, they remain an important component in learning. Since only the individual himself knows whether a skill needs more practice, the child must be given the freedom in a learning environment to practice a needed skill as much as he needs to. The implication of this is that the child sets his own pace for learning. Only he can tell when he is ready to move on to the next task. If the teacher tries to set the pace for him, she might deny him the practice he needs.

By the same token, the teacher must be sure that new materials are available, waiting for the child's signal that he is ready to move on. Montessori warned of the possibility that a child might stay with a well-versed skill after he is ready to progress if he is afraid of failing the next task or if there is no new task available. The teacher's role is crucial at this time. She must be a sensitive observer of her students. If the child's repetitive actions are rapid and efficient, she might try to attract him to a new activity. If, on the other hand, he is still gaining skill, she should not interfere with his learning.

In addition to repetition, imitation is an important tool in learning, readily observable in preschool children. Montessori believed in exploiting this tendency by allowing children the freedom of moving around the classroom whenever they choose and encouraging them to observe other children's activity. In many cases, a child might provide a better model for how to perform on some task than an adult can provide. If the child uses intermediate steps toward the solution that an adult might skip, or if the child's relatively poor dexterity requires a different movement than the adult with better coordination would make, then a child model will be better. Children are also more likely to exhibit incorrect problem-solving strategies which the observing child can himself avoid. Although children express the desire to be grown up and frequently imitate adults, they are also likely to imitate slightly older or more skillful children. The slightly older child provides a more realistic model in the sense that the younger child has a greater chance of being able to produce a reasonable approximation of the older child's actions. Montessori advocated having children of several different ages in one classroom just to facilitate imitation. If a particular school system will not permit mixing children of different ages, then at least teachers can avoid segregating the slower learners from the faster ones, and she can encourage the children to watch each other (without interfering, of course).

The recommendation to encourage imitation can be misinterpreted in two ways, both of which the reader is cautioned against. First, it does not mean that one particular child is identified as a star and held up as an example to the other children. No child wants to be reprimanded with "Why can't you behave or perform as well as sweet little Johnny?" The imitation recommended by Montessori and

Piaget is spontaneous in the sense of being child-initiated and springs from the observing child's desire to acquire a skill that he sees displayed by another child. Second, the recommendation for imitation should not be construed as a rejection of the importance of individual differences or creativity. Learning is an individual activity, paced by the child himself, and conducted according to his unique needs and prior experiences. The purpose of imitation is not to create similarity among children. Rather, it is to foster the learning of skills that is accomplished more slowly through direct tuition or through trial-and-error learning by the individual himself.

Despite encouraging imitation, Montessori classrooms are well known for their individual rather than group learning situations. If, as Montessori and Piaget believe, learning is self-motivated, individually paced, and dependent upon a unique combination of physical maturation and prior experiences, then no group activity will suit the needs of the individual children who comprise the group. Yet, if each child is engaged in a different activity, how can the teacher divide her time in a meaningful way among the children? Montessori's answer, to which Piaget would probably concur, is to provide instructional apparatus which the child can use without any assistance. A form board is a good example of such an apparatus. The child can learn about shapes by inserting pegs into their proper holes. Since the square peg will not fit into the round or triangular holes, the child can work on the task without a teacher standing over his shoulder telling him whether or not he made a mistake. Errors are obvious and so is success once it is achieved. Sizes, shapes, numbers, colors, pre-reading, and pre-writing skills are just some of the many things the pre-school child in a Montessori classroom can learn through self-instructional materials. There are other ways of setting up individual learning experiences (e.g., the Skinnerianbased teaching machines), but Montessori's system seems most compatible with Piaget's theory.

The reader should not infer that Piaget's theory is in perfect agreement with Montessori's educational philosophy. It is not. There is, for example, a fundamental disagreement over the importance of fantasy play for learning to separate make-believe from reality. The parallels drawn in this section should be viewed only as one of many possible ways of putting Piaget's theoretical ideas on cognitive development into educational practice.

SUMMARY

This chapter has indicated in a general fashion how Piaget's theory and the experimental research tradition can be useful to parents and educators. The philosophy expressed in both the parenting and educational sections was that children are fundamentally different from adults; therefore, what seems reasonable from an adult's perspective may seem completely unreasonable from a child's point of view, and vice versa. Both physical maturation and previous experience put limits on the child's capacity to learn. Sometimes those limitations are demonstrated when the child misbehaves; other times, the limitations show as a failure to profit from classroom instruction.

The characteristics of the Piagetian stages and the developmental advances in the processes of thought provide clues to parents concerning the reasons for their child's behavior. Many actions which are annoying might be slightly more tolerable if parents can figure out what problems their children are trying to solve. Teachers were also encouraged to analyze the tasks they demanded of their students. Successful learning is more likely to occur if the problem is within the child's perception, memory, and hypothesis-testing skills. Moreover, the problems are more likely to be solved if their elements are familiar to the child and if they are presented concretely rather than abstractly, at least for the elementary school and preschool child.

Parallels were drawn between Piaget's theory and the educational system of Maria Montessori. Both believe that children are intrinsically motivated to learn, that learning activities should be programmed to match the child's level of development, and that imitation and repetition are important aspects of learning.

183

REFERENCES

Adelson, J., & O'Neil, R. P. The growth of political ideas in adolescence: The sense of community. *Journal of Personality and Social Psychology*, 1966, *4*, 295-306.

Ault, R. L. Problem-solving strategies of reflective, impulsive, fast-accurate, and slow-inaccurate children. *Child Development*, 1973, *44*, 259-266.

Bernstein, A. C., & Cowan, P. A. Children's concepts of how people get babies. *Child Development*, 1975, *46*, 77-91.

Bower, T. G. R. The object in the world of the infant. *Scientific American*, 1971, *225*(4), 30-38.

Bruner, J. S. On perceptual readiness. *Psychological Review*, 1957, *64*, 123-152.

Bruner, J. S., Olver, R. R., & Greenfield, P. M. *Studies in cognitive growth*. New York: Wiley, 1966.

Caldwell, E. C., & Hall, V. C. Distinctive-features versus prototype learning reexamined. *Journal of Experimental Psychology*, 1970, *83*(1), 7-12.

Cohen, L. B. A two process model of infant visual attention. *Merrill-Palmer Quarterly*, 1973, *19*(3), 157-180.

Cohen, L. B., Gelber, E., & Lazar, M. Infant habituation and generalization to differing degrees of stimulus novelty. *Journal of Experimental Child Psychology*, 1971, *11*, 379-389.

Craik, F. I. M., & Lockhart, R. S. Levels of processing: A framework for memory research. *Journal of Verbal Learning and Verbal Behavior*, 1972, *11*, 671-684.

Craik, F. I. M., & Tulving, E. Depth of processing and the retention of words in episodic memory. *Journal of Experimental Psychology: General*, 1975, *104*, 268-294.

Debus, R. L. Effects of brief observation of model behavior on conceptual tempo of impulsive children. *Developmental Psychology,* 1970, *2,* 22-32.

Denney, D. R. Reflection and impulsivity as determinants of conceptual strategy. *Child Development,* 1973, *44,* 614-623.

Eimas, P. D. Effects of memory aids on hypothesis behavior and focusing in young children and adults. *Journal of Experimental Child Psychology,* 1970, *10,* 319-336.

Elkind, D. Children's discovery of the conservation of mass, weight, and volume: Piaget replication Study II. *The Journal of Genetic Psychology,* 1961, *98,* 219-227.

Elkind, D. Cognition in infancy and early childhood. In Y. Brackbill (Ed.), *Infancy and early childhood.* New York: Free Press, 1967. (a)

Elkind, D. Piaget and Montessori. *Harvard Educational Review,* 1967, *37,* 535-545. (b)

Elkind, D. *Children and adolescents: Interpretive essays on Jean Piaget.* New York: Oxford University Press, 1974.

Elkind, D. Perceptual development in children. *American Scientist,* 1975, *63*(5), 533-541.

Elkind, D., & Weiss, J. Studies in perceptual development III: Perceptual exploration. *Child Development,* 1967, *38,* 1153-1161.

Flavell, J. H. *The developmental psychology of Jean Piaget.* Princeton, N. J.: Van Nostrand, 1963.

Flavell, J. H. Stage-related properties of cognitive development. *Cognitive Psychology,* 1971, *2,* 421-453.

Flavell, J. H., Beach, D. R., & Chinsky, J. M. Spontaneous verbal rehearsal in a memory task as a function of age. *Child Development,* 1966, *37,* 283-299.

Furth, H. G. *Piaget and knowledge.* Englewood Cliffs, N.J.: Prentice-Hall, 1969.

Gelman, R. Conservation acquisition: A problem of learning to attend to relevant attributes. *Journal of Experimental Child Psychology,* 1969, *7,* 167-187.

Gibson, E. J. *Principles of perceptual learning and development.* New York: Appleton-Century-Crofts, 1969.

Ginsburg, H., & Opper, S. *Piaget's theory of intellectual development.* Englewood Cliffs, N.J.: Prentice-Hall, 1969.

Glick, J. Culture and cognition: Some theoretical and methodological concerns. Paper presented at the American Anthropological Association Meetings, New Orleans, November 1969.

Gollin, E. S. Developmental studies of visual recognition of incomplete pictures. *Perceptual and Motor Skills,* 1960, *11,* 289-298.

Gollin, E. S. Factors affecting the visual recognition of incomplete objects: A comparative investigation of children and adults. *Perceptual and Motor Skills,* 1962, *15,* 583-590.

Greenfield, P. M. Who is "Dada"? Some aspects of the semantic and phonological development of a child's first words. *Language and Speech,* 1973, *16,* 34-43.

Ingalls, R. P., & Dickerson, D. J. Development of hypothesis behavior in human concept identification. *Developmental Psychology,* 1969, *1,* 707-716.

Jeffrey, W. E. The orienting reflex and attention in cognitive development. *Psychological Review,* 1968, *75,* 323-334.

Kagan, J. A conception of early adolescence. *Daedalus,* 1971, *100*(4), 997-1012. (a)

Kagan, J. *Understanding children: Behavior, motives, and thought.* New York: Harcourt Brace Jovanovich, 1971. (b)

Kagan, J., Klein, R. E., Haith, M. M., & Morrison, F. J. Memory and meaning in two cultures. *Child Development,* 1973, *44,* 221-223.

Kagan, J., & Kogan, N. Individual variation in cognitive processes. In P. Mussen (Ed.), *Carmichael's manual of child psychology,* Vol. 1, New York: Wiley, 1970.

Kagan, J., Rosman, B. L., Day, D., Albert, J., & Phillips, W. Information processing in the child. *Psychological Monographs,* 1964, *78* (1, Whole No. 578).

Kesner, R. A neural system analysis of memory storage and retrieval. *Psychological Bulletin,* 1973, *80,* 177-203.

Kingsley, P. R., & Hagen, J. W. Induced versus spontaneous rehearsal in short-term memory in nursery school children. *Developmental Psychology,* 1969, *1,* 40-46.

Kingsley, R. C., & Hall, V. C. Training conservation through the use of learning sets. *Child Development,* 1967, *38,* 1111-1126.

Kreutzer, M. A., Leonard, Sister Catherine, & Flavell, J. H. An interview study of children's knowledge about memory. *Monographs of the Society for Research in Child Development,* 1975, *159*(1).

Levine, M. Hypothesis behavior by humans during discrimination learning. *Journal of Experimental Psychology,* 1966, *71,* 331-338.

Levine, M., Leitenberg, H., & Richter, M. The blank trials law: The equivalence of positive reinforcement and nonreinforcement. *Psychological Review,* 1964, *71,* 94-103.

McCall, R. B. Attention in the infant: Avenue to the study of cognitive development. In D. Walcher & D. Peters (Eds.), *Early childhood: The development of self-regulatory mechanisms.* New York: Academic, 1971.

McKinney, J. D., Haskins, R., & Mason, J. *Problem solving strategies in reflective and impulsive children* (Project No. 3-0344). Chapel Hill, North Carolina: Frank Porter Graham Child Development Center, August 1974.

Mehler, J., & Bever, T. G. Cognitive capacity of very young children. *Science,* 1967, *158,* 141-142.

Messer, S. B. The effect of anxiety over intellectual performance on reflection-impulsivity in children. *Child Development*, 1970, *41*, 723-735.

Miller, G. A. The magical number seven, plus or minus two: Some limits on our capacity for processing information. *Psychological Review*, 1956, *63*, 81-97.

Moely, B., Olson, P. A., Halwes, T. G., & Flavell, J. H. Production deficiency in young children's clustered recall. *Developmental Psychology*, 1969, *1*, 26-34.

Mosher, F. A., & Hornsby, J. R. On asking questions. In J. S. Bruner, R. R. Olver, & P. M. Greenfield (Eds.), *Studies in cognitive growth*. New York: Wiley, 1966.

Mussen, P. H., Conger, J. J., & Kagan, J. *Child development and personality*. New York: Harper & Row, 1974.

Olver, R. R., & Hornsby, J. R. On equivalence. In J. S. Bruner, R. R. Olver, & P. M. Greenfield (Eds.), *Studies in cognitive growth*. New York: Wiley, 1966.

Piaget, J. *The child's conception of the world*. New York: Harcourt, Brace, and World, 1929.

Piaget, J. *The child's conception of physical causality*. London: Kegan Paul, 1930.

Posner, M. I. *Cognition: An introduction*. Glenview, Ill.: Scott, Foresman, 1973.

Ridberg, E. H., Parke, R. D., & Hetherington, E. M. Modification of impulsive and reflective cognitive styles through observation of film-mediated models. *Developmental Psychology*, 1971, *5*, 369-377.

Santostefano, S., & Paley, E. Development of cognitive controls in children. *Child Development*, 1964, *35*, 939-949.

Smedslund, J. Transitivity of preference patterns as seen by preschool children. *Scandinavian Journal of Psychology*, 1960, *1*, 49-54.

Sperling, G. The information available in brief visual presentations. *Psychological Monographs*, 1960, *74* (Whole No. 11).

Stevenson, H. W. *Children's learning*. New York: Appleton-Century-Crofts, 1972.

Stroop, J. R. Studies of interference in serial verbal reactions. *Journal of Experimental Psychology*, 1935, *18*, 643-662.

Van Horn, K. R., & Bartz, W. H. Information seeking strategies in cognitive development. *Psychonomic Science*, 1968, *11*, 341-342.

Vernon, M. D. The functions of schemata in perceiving. *Psychological Review*, 1955, *62*, 180-192.

Webster's New World Dictionary of the American Language (College edition). New York: The World Publishing Company, 1960.

Weir, M. W. Developmental changes in problem-solving strategies. *Psychological Review*, 1964, *71*, 473-490.

Weizenbaum, J. Contextual understanding by computers. In P. A. Kolers & M. Eden (Eds.), *Recognizing patterns: Studies in living and automatic systems*. Cambridge, Mass.: M.I.T. Press, 1968.

Schema hypothesis, see Perception, enrichment theory
Scheme (pl: schemes), 18-21, 28, 31, 32-35, 47, 82, 85, 145, 146, 152, 157, 162
Search for hidden objects, see Object permanence; Symbolic functions
Selective attention, see Attention, selectivity of
Sensorimotor Period, 22-47, 82, 141, 151, 159, 177, 179
Stage 1: 27, 34, 151
Stage 2: 28, 34, 179
Stage 3: 29, 30, 34, 179
Stage 4: 31, 34
Stage 5: 32, 34, 159, 179
Stage 6: 33, 34
see also Infancy
Sensory memory, see Memory storage systems
Sensory systems, 23-25
Sequential development, see Stage theory
Short-term memory, see Memory storage systems
Smedslund, J., 66
Specific hypothesis question, see Twenty Questions
Sperling, G., 107, 108
Stage, 8, 9, 16, 21, 22, 77, 78, 80, 82, 138, 139, 156, 160, 183
see also Object permanence; Sensorimotor Period
Stage theory, 22, 78-81, 139-142, 144
invariance of order, 80, 81, 139, 178
irreversibility, 78, 81
sequential development, 78, 156, 178
Stanford-Binet Intelligence Test, 137

Status, see Concept, developmental changes in
Stevenson, H. W., 15, 105, 125
Stroop, J. R., 100, 101
Symbol, 84, 88, 89, 97, 99, 133, 135, 152, 163
see also Units of thought
Symbolic functions, 23, 47-49, 53, 61, 82, 88
Symbolic play, 20, 21, 48, 49, 163, 182

Trial-and-error learning, 32, 33, 73, 75, 166, 181
Tulving, E., 118
Twenty Questions, 90-92, 121-123, 131, 135, 148, 166, 175

Units of thought, 85-97, 119, 133-135, 151, 156
see also Concept; Rule; Schema; Symbol

Validity, see Concept, developmental changes in
Van Horn, K. R., 92, 170
Vernon, M. D., 102
Vocabulary development, see Language

Weir, M. W., 124
Weiss, J., 173
Weizenbaum, J., 169